Teacher's Resource Guide

Reading and Writing for Today's Adults

Voyager

4
5
6

Advisers to the Series

Mary Dunn Siedow
Director
North Carolina Literacy Resource Center
Raleigh, NC

Linda Thistlethwaite
Associate Director
The Central Illinois Adult Education Service Center
Western Illinois University
Macomb, IL

New Readers Press

Contributing Writers

Book 4 Teacher's Notes: Cathy Niemet

Books 5 and 6 Teacher's Notes: Sarah Conroy Williams

Voyager: Reading and Writing for Today's Adults™ Teacher's Resource Guide for Voyager 4–6
ISBN 1-56420-170-8
Copyright © 1999
New Readers Press
U.S. Publishing Division of Laubach Literacy International
Box 131, Syracuse, New York 13210-0131

Printed in the United States of America
9 8 7 6 5 4 3

Director of Acquisitions and Development: Christina Jagger
Content Editor: Mary Hutchison
Developer: Learning Unlimited, Oak Park, IL
Developmental Editor: Pamela Bliss
Production Director: Jennifer Lohr
Cover Designer: Gerald Russell
Copy Editor: Judi Lauber
Designer: Kimbrly Koennecke

Contents

Overview of the Series

Voyager: Reading and Writing for Today's Adults is a four-stage program that utilizes contemporary content and instructional approaches to teach the reading, writing, critical thinking, and communication skills that adults need in today's world. It takes students from the beginning stages of reading and writing through the ninth-grade level.

The *Voyager* series consists of nine student books, nine workbooks, four teacher's resource guides, and a placement tool.

▶ Key Features and Benefits

1. ***Voyager* integrates contemporary content and instructional approaches with the best elements from traditional instruction and practice.** In the early books, phonics and other word recognition strategies are combined with reading comprehension instruction. Later books emphasize comprehension and meaning. Instruction in the writing process is combined with instruction in spelling, capitalization, punctuation, grammar, usage, and sentence structure. This balanced approach results in a solid, effective program.

2. **Each lesson integrates reading, writing, listening, speaking, and thinking skills.** Research has shown that literacy development is enhanced when students have the opportunity to apply all these skills to a single topic. Activities and skill-building exercises in *Voyager* are related to the topic of the reading selection, the core of the lesson.

3. ***Voyager* is theme-based.** In *Foundation Book,* each lesson has a theme. The other eight student books are divided into four units, each with its own theme. This theme-based approach encourages students to delve into a topic using a variety of approaches. As students complete the reading, writing, and thinking activities in a unit, they have opportunities to examine the common concepts and issues associated with that unit's theme.

4. **Students work with authentic reading selections and writing assignments—practical, informational, and literary.** *Voyager* draws from a combination of high-quality literature, information-rich articles, adult student writings, and the types of forms, documents, and graphic material adults commonly encounter. Working with these materials, students achieve success at both academic and everyday reading and writing activities.

5. **Activities in *Voyager* give students opportunities to work both independently and collaboratively.** Students complete some activities by themselves. In other activities, students participate in discussions, group problem solving, and so on. These varied ways of working reflect daily life.

6. ***Voyager* can be successfully used in a variety of settings.** *Voyager* can be used in large- or small-group instructional programs, in one-on-one tutorial situations, and independently for self-study in an individualized or learning lab program. This flexible instructional format meets the needs of a wide variety of programs.

7. ***Voyager* provides additional support for both students and teachers.** Workbooks, to be used independently by students, are filled with exercises that give them extra practice with the major skills taught in the lessons. Teacher's resource guides provide valuable additional background information, teaching ideas, and photocopy masters (PCMs). These support materials save time by helping teachers create lesson plans and reinforcement materials.

▶ A Closer Look at *Voyager* Components

▶ **Nine student books** form the instructional core of the *Voyager* program.

▶ **Nine workbooks,** one for each student book, provide students with extra skills practice.

▶ **Four teacher's resource guides,** one for each stage, contain a general overview and orientation to each stage, lesson-by-lesson teacher's notes and extension activities for the student books, and PCMs for both instruction and assessment.

▶ **The placement tool** helps teachers place students in the appropriate *Voyager* student book.

The Four Stages

The *Voyager* series is a four-stage program. Each stage of *Voyager* reflects a separate stage of reading and writing development. Thus, each stage has its own emphasis and design. The four stages are

1. **Learning to Read** (Reading levels 0.5–2.5) Emphasis at this stage is on short reading selections containing common words; phonics instruction; and writing, speaking, and listening activities to teach basic skills and build confidence.

2. **The Emerging Reader** (Reading levels 2.0–4.5) Emphasis at this stage is on literary and informational reading selections; phonics and other word recognition strategies; comprehension and critical-thinking strategies; and writing, speaking, and listening skills.

3. **Reading to Learn** (Reading levels 4.0–7.5) Emphasis at this stage is on expanding students' reading, thinking, writing, and oral communication skills, using reading materials typically found at home, at work, at school, and in the community.

4. **Reading for Work and Life** (Reading levels 7.0–9.5) Emphasis at this stage is on having students learn and apply reading, thinking, writing, and oral communication skills through themes and readings that are work- and life-oriented.

Components of the *Voyager* Series

Stages	Student Books (96 – 176 pages)	Reading Levels	Workbooks (48 pages each)	Teacher's Resource Guides
Learning to Read	Voyager Foundation Book (96 pages)	0.5 – 1.5	Voyager Foundation Workbook	Teacher's Resource Guide for Foundation Book and Voyager 1 (80 pages)
	Voyager 1 (128 pages)	1.0 – 2.5	Voyager 1 Workbook	
The Emerging Reader	Voyager 2 (128 pages)	2.0 – 3.5	Voyager 2 Workbook	Teacher's Resource Guide for Voyager 2 and 3 (80 pages)
	Voyager 3 (128 pages)	3.0 – 4.5	Voyager 3 Workbook	
Reading to Learn	Voyager 4 (160 pages)	4.0 – 5.5	Voyager 4 Workbook	Teacher's Resource Guide for Voyager 4 – 6 (96 pages)
	Voyager 5 (160 pages)	5.0 – 6.5	Voyager 5 Workbook	
	Voyager 6 (160 pages)	6.0 – 7.5	Voyager 6 Workbook	
Reading for Work and Life	Voyager 7 (176 pages)	7.0 – 8.5	Voyager 7 Workbook	Teacher's Resource Guide for Voyager 7 and 8 (80 pages)
	Voyager 8 (176 pages)	8.0 – 9.5	Voyager 8 Workbook	

▶ A Closer Look at the Student Books

Voyager contains nine student books.

Foundation Book

The first book is *Foundation Book*. This book has 28 lessons divided into five units. Units 1–3 contain 18 lessons and introduce the sounds and names of single consonants. Unit 4 contains five lessons that introduce the five vowels and the short vowel sounds in a word-family context. Unit 5 contains five lessons introducing common initial consonant blends.

The activities in each lesson give students opportunities to generate words containing the target letters and sounds, and to read and write sentences or stories that contain words with those letters and sounds. The lessons also include activities to build listening, speaking, and critical-thinking skills.

Student Books 1–8

▶ **Units:** Student books 1–8 are each divided into four units organized around themes relevant to adult life, such as Hopes and Dreams, Express Yourself, On the Job, and Resolving Conflict. Each unit contains three lessons in which students explore different aspects of the theme while working with activities that integrate reading, writing, listening, speaking, and thinking skills.

Each unit ends with (1) a one-page Writing Skills Mini-Lesson that teaches a specific writing skill, such as capitalization, and (2) a cumulative unit review that covers the main skills taught in the unit.

▶ **Lessons:** Lessons in student books 1–8 contain the following features:

Pre-Reading Activities: Each lesson begins with a pre-reading activity designed to activate student interest and prior knowledge, or to teach information needed to understand the reading at the heart of the lesson.

Reading Selections: Over the course of the series, students are exposed to a wide variety of authentic, high-quality reading selections. The readings are a rich mixture of short stories; poetry; drama; essays; adult student writings; informational pieces; and common documents, forms, and graphics.

Post-Reading Activities: Through activities related to the reading selection and the unit's theme, students develop their vocabulary, comprehension, and higher-order thinking skills; build their writing competence; and work to master common documents, forms, and graphics. The blend of these features depends on the level of the book.

▶ **Assessment:** Each book begins with a Skills Preview and ends with a cumulative Skills Review. Books 1–6 also contain student self-assessments to use before beginning and after completing each book.

▶ **Answer Key and Reference Handbook:** Students can find an answer key and a reference handbook at the back of each book.

The diagram below shows the organization of Books 1–8.

Organization of *Voyager* Books 1-8

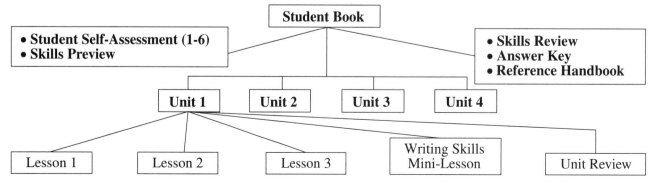

▶ A Closer Look at Assessment

Assessment in *Voyager* is based on these principles:

1. **Assessment should inform instruction.** Assessment can monitor a student's progress, provide feedback and a framework for remediation, and determine mastery.
2. **Assessment should allow learners to express expectations and evaluate progress.** Specific instruments can help students express their goals and needs and evaluate what they have learned.
3. **Assessment should allow for measurement and documentation of a student's progress and educational gains.** Such documentation is essential for students, teachers, and schools.

Series Assessment Tools

This program provides these assessment tools:

- The **Placement Tool** will help you to place a student in the appropriate *Voyager* student book.
- **Student Interest Inventories** in Books 1–3 and **Student Self-Assessments** in Books 4–6 let students evaluate their level of activity and proficiency with various reading and writing tasks.
- The **Skills Preview** in each student book tests students' proficiency with the reading and writing tasks to be covered in the book.
- **Unit Reviews** test the key skills in the unit.
- The **Skills Review** in each student book tests the key reading and writing skills taught in the entire book.

Alternative Assessment Tools

You can utilize any of the following alternative assessment instruments with *Voyager.*

▶ Writing

Dialogue Journals: A student writes observations and ideas in a journal on an ongoing basis, and the teacher responds in the journal (see page 20).

Writing Portfolios: These are collections of student writings (see page 20).

▶ Personal Progress Portfolios

Working Folders: Students date and keep all their works-in-progress and finished work in their working folders. They also keep their "Student Progress Tracking Sheets" in this folder.

Progress Portfolios: Progress Portfolios let students demonstrate progress over time. PCMs have instructions for helping *Voyager* students evaluate the material in their working folders and assemble Progress Portfolios.

▶ Evaluation

Student conferences allow you to evaluate a student's portfolio. These conferences should help students to see their progress as well as show them areas that need improvement. A PCM is provided as a guide for conducting these conferences.

Main Purposes of Voyager Assessment Tools

	Inform Instructor	Empower Learner	Measure Progress
Series Assessments			
Placement Tool	X		
Student Interest Inventory		X	X
Skills Preview	X	X	X
Unit Review	X	X	X
Skills Review	X	X	X
Alternative Assessments			
Dialogue Journal	X	X	
Writing Portfolio	X	X	X
Personal Progress Portfolio	X	X	X

Voyager 4 Scope and Sequence

Unit	Lesson	Reading Selection	Genre	Reading Strategy
Unit 1: Staying Healthy	1	"I've Got to Change"	Fiction	Use your prior experience
	2	"Eat More Fruits & Vegetables"	Pamphlet	Set a purpose
	3	"How to Avoid Food That Makes You Sick"	Article	Predict content
	Writing Skills Mini-Lesson			
	Unit 1 Review			
Unit 2: Get That Job!	4	"Easy Job, Good Wages"	Fiction	Visualize
	5	"Determined to Find a Job"	Scenario and job application	Predict features
	6	"Tips for Job Hunting"	Article	Use your prior knowledge
	Writing Skills Mini-Lesson			
	Unit 2 Review			
Unit 3: A Sense of Community	7	"Make Sure What You're Looking at Is Really What You See"	Adult student writing	Use your prior experience
	8	"Let's Go Out"	Scenario and map	Predict features
	9	"Your Library: A Major Community Resource"	Brochure	Predict content
	Writing Skills Mini-Lesson			
	Unit 3 Review			
Unit 4: Crime and the Law	10	"Three 'Little' People Who Changed U.S. History"	Article	Use your prior knowledge
	11	"Americans Held Hostage"	Political cartoon and letters to the editor	Set a purpose
	12	"Crimebusters"	Fiction	Visualize
	Writing Skills Mini-Lesson			
	Unit 4 Review			

Reading and Thinking Skill	Writing	Speaking and Listening	Life Skill	TRG pages	Workbook pages
Recognize problems and solutions	Write a descriptive paragraph	Discuss	Read medicine labels	22–24	4–5
Apply information	Fill in a KWL chart	Discuss	Read a chart	24–25	6
Understand cause and effect	Create a chart	Ask questions	Fill in a medical history form	25–26	7–8
	Fix sentence fragments			26	9
				26	10–13
Understand cause and effect	Write a descriptive paragraph	Retell	Interpret newspaper want ads	27–28	14–15
Locate key facts	Fill in a personal information sheet	Discuss	Fill in a job application form	28–29	16
Identify the main idea	Write about an interesting job	Role-play	Fill in a job network web	29–30	17–18
	Fix run-on sentences			31	19
				31	20–23
Recognize problems and solutions	Write about a problem and a solution	Discuss	Use a phone book	32–33	24–25
Follow directions	Write directions	Give directions	Draw a map	33–34	26
Locate key facts	Write an announcement	Use telephone skills	Use the library	34–35	27–28
	Correct usage problems			35–36	29
				36	30–33
Apply information	Write your opinion	Discuss	Read a bar graph	37–38	34–35
Identify the main idea	Write a letter to the editor	Discuss	Analyze a political cartoon	38–39	36
Follow a sequence of events	Write a poem	Retell	Read a parking ticket	39–40	37–38
	Use apostrophes correctly			41	39
				41	40–43

Voyager 5 Scope and Sequence

Unit	Lesson	Reading Selection	Genre	Reading Strategy
Unit 1: Money Matters	1	"What's Eating Your Paycheck?"	Article	Set a purpose
	2	"Opening a Checking Account"	Scenario, chart, and bank signature card	Skim
	3	"$100 Dreams"	Article	Use your prior experience
	Writing Skills Mini-Lesson			
	Unit 1 Review			
Unit 2: On the Job	4	"I'm Not Making Coffee" and others	Adult student writing and poem	Imagine
	5	"First Day on the Job"	Scenario, work order, and diagram	Use your prior experience
	6	"Problem Solving on the Job"	Memos	Use your prior knowledge
	Writing Skills Mini-Lesson			
	Unit 2 Review			
Unit 3: Making a Difference	7	"Shirley Chisholm"	Biography	Predict content
	8	"A New Voter in the West End"	Scenario and voter registration form	Skim
	9	"Volunteers in Schools"	Letters to the editor	Use your prior knowledge
	Writing Skills Mini-Lesson			
	Unit 3 Review			
Unit 4: Many Cultures	10	"The Eagle and the Spider" and others	Fables	Imagine
	11	"No Words to Say Good-bye"	Diary	Use your prior experience
	12	"The Struggle to Be an All-American Girl"	Essay	Set a purpose
	Writing Skills Mini-Lesson			
	Unit 4 Review			

Reading and Thinking Skill	Writing	Speaking and Listening	Life Skill	TRG pages	Workbook pages
Identify the main idea and details	Write an action plan	Summarize	Read a circle graph	43–44	4–5
Understand categories	Fill in a bank signature card	Role-play	Read a bank statement	44–45	6
Recognize problems and solutions	Write a short article	Interview	Understand a budget	45–47	7–8
	Capitalization rules			47	9
				47	10–13
Make inferences	Write a personal account	Discuss	Read workplace signs and symbols	48–49	14–15
Follow steps in a process	Write directions	Discuss	Read a diagram	49–50	16
Identify facts and opinions	Write a memo	Summarize	Read a time sheet and an invoice	51	17–18
	Subject-verb agreement			51–52	19
				52	20–23
Summarize information	Write an autobiography	Tell about someone	Read a brochure	53–55	24–25
Categorize information	Write a persuasive letter	Interview	Read community announcements	55–56	26
Identify facts and opinions	Write a letter to the editor	Discuss	Read bar graphs	56–57	27–28
	More on subject-verb agreement			57	29
				57	30–33
Compare and contrast	Write a fable	Tell a story	Read a map	58–60	34–35
Make inferences	Write a diary entry	Discuss	Read a schedule	60–61	36
Identify the main idea and details	Write an essay	Summarize	Read a chart	61–62	37–38
	Combining ideas			62	39
				62–63	40–43

Voyager 6 Scope and Sequence

Unit	Lesson	Reading Selection	Genre	Reading Strategy
Unit 1: Success at Work	1	"The Deli"	Personal account	Empathize
	2	"Evaluation Time"	Scenario and performance evaluations	Use your prior experience
	3	"How to Be Successful at Work"	Article	Skim
	Writing Skills Mini-Lesson			
	Unit 1 Review			
Unit 2: Taking a Stand	4	"The Right Thing to Do at the Time"	Story	Use your prior knowledge
	5	"Extraordinary People"	Biographical sketches	Predict content
	6	"I Have a Dream"	Speech	Use your prior knowledge
	Writing Skills Mini-Lesson			
	Unit 2 Review			
Unit 3: Relationships	7	"On Golden Pond"	Drama	Visualize
	8	"The Corn Planting"	Fiction	Imagine
	9	"Recent Trends in U.S. Living Arrangements"	Bar graphs	Use your prior knowledge
	Writing Skills Mini-Lesson			
	Unit 3 Review			
Unit 4: Insights	10	"The Story of My Life"	Autobiography	Imagine
	11	"A Fear I Had"	Adult student writing	Empathize
	12	"A Success as a Teacher and Builder"	Biographical article	Use your prior experience
	Writing Skills Mini-Lesson			
	Unit 4 Review			

Reading and Thinking Skill	Writing	Speaking and Listening	Life Skill	TRG pages	Workbook pages
Understand cause and effect	Explain how to do something	Summarize	Read a paycheck stub	65–66	4–5
Identify facts and opinions	Write a performance evaluation	Role-play	Fill in a vacation request form	66–67	6
Identify the main idea and details	Write a business letter	Discuss	Read a bar graph	67–68	7–8
	Subject-verb agreement: *be* and *have*			68–69	9
				69	10–13
Identify theme	Write about an incident	Discuss	Read a political cartoon	70–71	14–15
Compare and contrast	Write a biographical sketch	Summarize	Read a map	71–72	16–17
Identify the main idea and details	Write an opinion	Read aloud	Read a line graph	72–73	18
	Commas in compound sentences			73	19
				74	20–23
Make inferences	Write dialogue	Read aloud	Read a map	75–76	24–25
Identify theme	Write a friendly letter	Discuss	Read a family tree	76–77	26–27
Identify facts and opinions	Write your opinion	Discuss	Read a double line graph	77–78	28
	Complex sentences			78	29
				78–79	30–33
Make inferences	Write the results of an interview	Discuss	Read a time line	80–81	34–35
Compare and contrast	Compare and contrast two things	Discuss	Fill in a hospital admission form	81–82	36–37
Understand cause-and-effect chains	Write a cause-and-effect paragraph	Tell a story	Read a circle graph	82–84	38
	Pronoun problems			84	39
				84	40–43

Overview of *Voyager 4, Voyager 5,* and *Voyager 6*

▶ Parts of the Books

Voyager 4, Voyager 5, and *Voyager 6* are each divided into four theme-based units to give students a meaningful context for their reading, writing, thinking, listening, and speaking activities.

The Four Units

Below is an overview of unit features in *Voyager 4, 5,* and *6.* Details and tips for teaching the lessons are in the Teacher's Notes (pages 21–84).

Unit Overviews The overview introduces the theme of the unit. The readings and activities throughout a unit are related to its theme.

Lessons Each unit has three lessons. Each lesson contains these features:

- **Learning Goals** a list of the main objectives of each lesson. Knowing the goals empowers students to take charge of the learning process.
- **Before You Read** a strategy to help students prepare for the reading selection. Students are encouraged to think about their own knowledge of or experience with the reading topic, or they are given essential background information.
- **Preview the Reading** suggestions for scanning the reading selection to get a sense of what the reading will be about
- **Use the Strategy** a reminder, to help students apply the reading strategy
- **Reading** a story, article, biography, essay, poem, or letter relating to the unit's theme
- **After You Read** questions, activities, and discussion topics to check students' comprehension of and reaction to the reading selection
- **Think About It** instruction and practice in a targeted reading and thinking skill
- **Write About It** instruction and guided practice in producing a piece of writing
- **Life Skill** instruction and practice in such everyday tasks as filling in forms and reading graphs, labels, and diagrams

Writing Skills Mini-Lessons Each unit has a one-page mini-lesson after the last lesson. The mini-lessons explore a particular issue of mechanics or sentence structure to help students master basic conventions of written English.

Unit Reviews The unit reviews recap the reading and writing activities in each unit. The writing process is introduced and used with one of the drafts written during the unit.

Before Starting the Units

Student Self-Assessment This assessment tool lets students evaluate their current level of activity and proficiency with a variety of everyday reading and writing tasks. Although it is self-assessment, you will need to work through it with each student.

Skills Preview The Skills Preview helps you diagnose how well students read independently and how well they write on a given topic.

While Working through the Units

Answer Key The Answer Key provides answers to exercises in the lessons, Writing Skills Mini-Lessons, and unit reviews.

Reference Handbook This handbook contains
- **Writing Skills:** a summary of the information in the mini-lessons
- **The Writing Process:** an outline of the five stages of the writing process

After Working through the Units

Skills Review The Skills Review is a cumulative review of the skills taught in *Voyager 4, 5,* or *6.* If students do well on the Skills Review, you should feel comfortable moving them on to the next *Voyager* book.

▶ How to Use *Voyager 4, 5, and 6*

You can use *Voyager 4, 5, and 6* for one-on-one or group instruction. The Teacher's Notes that start on page 21 will guide you through each lesson in these books. You may adapt these notes to fit your specific needs.

Before you begin, read the "Suggestions for Teaching *Voyager 4, 5, and 6*" on page 17. This material gives insight into the special needs of adult literacy students. It suggests specific strategies that have proven successful with adult students.

Begin your work by discussing students' educational goals with them. Describe ways in which you will help them reach those goals. Work through the assessment materials at the beginning of the book with each student to assess individual skill levels and needs.

As you work through *Voyager* with students, assess what material each student can do independently and on what type of material he or she needs guidance. Encourage as much independence as possible, but be careful not to frustrate students by having unrealistic expectations.

Adult students need a lot of feedback. Focus on the positive—what students have learned or accomplished. Keep in mind, however, that adult students can also detect insincere praise, so be positive, but truthful.

Working with a Range of Students in a Group Setting

If you are involved in group instruction, your students' literacy levels may vary. Students may range from those who are relatively new to reading to those who need just a review before moving on. It is essential that you get to know your students as individuals with specific interests and skill levels.

Although students may be placed in a group based on their assessed reading level, you will find that adult students have diverse skills and skill levels. The following strategies can be used with a mixed-ability group:

- Work through the first unit of the *Voyager* book with the entire class. If some students move quickly through the material on their own, let those students work ahead in a lesson independently, drawing them back for small- and whole-group discussions, such as Talk About It, and for peer review of writing assignments.
- Involve more able students in peer tutoring. For instance, have students read to each other and review each other's writing and practice work.
- The more able students can do reinforcement and extension activities while the rest of the group finishes a lesson. They can complete the workbook pages that accompany the student book lesson. The workbook exercises are designed to be done independently and should not require teacher input. Extension activities are suggested in the Teacher's Notes.

Using the Student Self-Assessments

Before students begin *Voyager 4, 5,* or *6,* ask them to complete Student Self-Assessment #1. Point out that it will help you get to know the student better and will give the student a way to evaluate his or her progress over time. You may need to explain the meaning of some terms, especially in the section called "When I read, I can . . ." Then discuss each student's completed checklist individually. Use the checklist as a way for students to set goals for learning.

When students have finished the *Voyager* book, have them complete Student Self-Assessment #2 and compare this checklist with their answers on Self-Assessment #1. Discuss their progress and their ongoing goals.

Using the Skills Preview

Have students complete the Skills Preview independently. Allow plenty of time. Use the Skills Preview Answers and the Skills Chart to get a sense of the student's comfort level with material taught in that particular *Voyager* book. Discuss the results with the student.

If a student has great difficulty with the Skills Preview, consider using the previous *Voyager* book instead. Conversely, if a student has little or no difficulty, you can have the student complete the Skills Review. If this is also easily completed, consider using the next level *Voyager* book.

Working through the Lessons

The Teacher's Notes on pages 21–84 provide teaching suggestions for each lesson in *Voyager 4, 5,* and *6.*

Working with the Reading Selections

The reading selection is the heart of each lesson. Read the title aloud. Ask students to look at the art. Ask what they think the reading will be about. You can use the following strategies to help students better understand the reading.

- Guide students through Before You Read. Assure them that there are no right or wrong answers to these pre-reading activities. These activities both help them tap into knowledge they already have and also provide information they may need to fully understand the selection.
- Have students follow the instructions in Preview the Reading. By skimming the selection and noting any headings and illustrations, students will get an idea of the content, which helps promote comprehension.
- Be sure to have students use the Check-ins in the margins as reminders that they need to understand the previous content before going on. The Check-ins ask students to apply the reading strategy introduced in Before You Read. In the beginning lessons, suggest that students note in the margins or on separate paper their answers to Check-in questions. With practice, the use of the reading strategies should become second nature to students.
- Students should read silently most of the time. However, both you and the students should read aloud occasionally. When you read aloud, you model the fluency, pace, and inflections of good reading. When students read aloud, they build their oral reading skills. When asking students to read aloud, always give them a chance to read

the selection silently first to gain confidence with the material.

- As students read, they may stumble on unfamiliar words. In *Voyager 4, 5,* and *6,* some of the difficult words are defined at the bottom of the page. Explain how to use footnotes. If students have trouble with a word that is not defined, encourage them to try to figure out the word from the context. For other decoding strategies, see PCM 8: Strategies for Recognizing Words.

Using the Answer Key

Encourage students to check and correct their own work. You should also check students' answers as they complete an exercise or lesson.

Using the Reference Handbook

You and your students can refer to the Reference Handbook at any time during *Voyager* instruction. Here are some tips:

- **Writing Skills** Have students refer to these pages whenever they are editing their writing.
- **The Writing Process** Refer students to this page when you introduce the writing process and whenever they do the writing portion of a unit review.

Using the Skills Review

Have students complete the Skills Review independently. Use the Skills Review Answers and the Evaluation Chart to help students evaluate their performance. Read what students wrote in the Write About It section, and give them feedback on all parts of the writing process.

Discuss the results with students. If a student struggled through or performed poorly on a section of the Skills Review, assess any problem areas. You may want the student to review the lessons or units in which these areas are covered before moving on to the next *Voyager* book.

Finally, have students fill in Student Self-Assessment #2. Discuss their progress and ongoing goals.

Suggestions for Teaching
Voyager 4, Voyager 5, and *Voyager 6*

▶ Purpose of *Voyager 4, 5,* and *6*

Voyager 4, 5, and *6* continue the *Voyager* approach of immersing students in the reading and writing processes. Students use reading strategies to help improve their reading comprehension. They analyze and discuss reading selections and practice such higher-order thinking skills as recognizing fact and opinion, applying information, inferring, and comparing and contrasting. Students use the writing process as they develop their writing skills. Students also develop real-life competencies such as reading schedules, graphs, and medicine labels.

After successfully completing these three books, students will have learned to
- work through theme-based units
- read various literary genres such as fiction, biography, essays, articles, drama, and poetry
- use a variety of reading strategies and skills to improve comprehension
- apply higher-order reading and thinking skills
- use the writing process to write letters, articles, stories, sketches, and other pieces
- read and interpret real-life materials such as forms, maps, diagrams, and charts

▶ Characteristics of Adult Learners

When working through these or other materials, keep in mind the following characteristics common to adult students:

Adult learners	As a teacher or tutor of adult learners, you should
want and deserve respect but may fear school	• stress accomplishments • give frequent praise • emphasize skills students already have
have a wealth of life experience	• emphasize how much students already can do • design some activities around students' interests and experiences
want to apply what they learn but may feel insecure about using new skills	• provide many opportunities for practice • model and/or practice skills before having students work independently
are accustomed to making decisions	• involve students in setting goals and objectives • offer choices of activities • respect the students' priorities
are busy people and may find planning for the future difficult	• help students prioritize learning goals • develop supplemental activities that speak to special interests • use time carefully

Adapted from *Teaching Adults: A Literacy Resource Book,* New Readers Press, 1994

▶ Working with Adult Student Readers

Voyager has been developed to help adult learners build their reading and writing skills. You can use a variety of strategies to help students build their reading skills and their self-confidence. Here are suggestions in four key areas: comprehension, decoding skills, life skills, and fluency.

Improving Comprehension

Even if students can read all the words in a passage, they may not understand the meaning of the whole passage. Or they may understand on a literal level, but not on a higher level of comprehension. Developing students' ability to infer, analyze, and evaluate is key to building their ability to fully comprehend and appreciate a reading selection. Experience and research have shown that students get more out of reading if they use strategies that engage them actively in the reading process, for example:

- **Pre-reading strategies** include setting a purpose for reading, activating prior knowledge and experience, skimming, and acquiring necessary background knowledge. In addition to the pre-reading activities in the student books, using graphic organizers encourages active reading. (See, for example, PCM 1: KWHL Chart.)
- **During-reading strategies** include predicting what might happen next, visualizing characters and settings, and empathizing with the characters. Check-ins remind students to apply these strategies as they read.
- **Post-reading strategies** Skill-building activities in Think About It are designed to help students develop such higher-order comprehension skills as identifying main ideas and details, inferring, recognizing cause and effect, locating key facts, applying information, and identifying problems and solutions. The Teacher's Notes in this book suggest ideas for practicing and extending the skill taught in each lesson.

Improving Decoding and Word Recognition Skills

Students reading at levels 4–6 have a fairly large sight vocabulary and can decode many unfamiliar

words. However, they need to continue developing their decoding skills. Here are some tools to use in helping them build those skills:

- **PCM 8: Strategies for Recognizing Words** This resource offers tips for decoding and recognizing unfamiliar words. The tips include using context clues and structural analysis (dividing longer words into their component parts). You can use PCM 8 whenever students need to practice these skills.
- **Published dictionaries** It is important to determine if students know how to use a dictionary. If some students have not used a dictionary, teach them how to use the guide words to find words. Give them practice looking up words, using pronunciation guides, and reading definitions. (Select words from the student book lessons, or create your own lists.) Use words in sentences to give students practice in selecting the definition that fits a specific context.
- **Personal dictionaries** Students can develop their own dictionaries to help them learn sight words. Have them label each page of a notebook with a letter of the alphabet. They can write a word they want to learn and a sentence containing that word on the appropriate page. Students can also create special pages for different contexts, such as work, school, family, or other topics that interest them.

Improving Life Skills Reading

Life skills reading refers to the written material that we must read and interpret daily. This broad category includes phone books, medicine labels, signs and symbols, bank statements, diagrams, maps, graphs, job application forms, want ads, and other such materials. To master life skills materials, students must both understand the information and also apply it to their own lives. For instance, students need to be able to read the information on a bottle of aspirin, and then take the prescribed dosage.

Each lesson in *Voyager 4, 5,* and *6* provides practice with a particular type of life skills reading. A wide variety of material is presented. In addition, you and your students can build a collection of life skills reading specifically relevant to their lives. Ask students to bring in reading materials they feel are important. The materials may be job-related (e.g., their weekly schedule or a copy of an important memo); financial (e.g., blank credit card applications); medical (e.g., an insurance form); or anything else your students need to use. You can develop activities with the materials, but be sure to delete any personal information first.

Improving Fluency

Independent Reading The more students read, the more fluent they will become. In addition to working through *Voyager,* adult students should be exposed to a wide variety of other reading materials—magazine articles, stories, newspapers, and so forth. Many public libraries have materials for adults with limited reading skills. You can also get the weekly newspaper *News for You,* as well as high-interest, low-reading-level books—both fiction and informative reading—from New Readers Press.

Reading Aloud Regular practice in reading aloud will help students develop oral reading fluency. After they have read a selection silently, you can have volunteers read aloud part or all of the selection, depending on its length.

► Working with Adult Student Writers

Accomplished writers have generally gained control over the mechanics of writing and can concentrate on the composing aspects. Adult student writers, however, still struggle with both aspects of writing. Here are some strategies to help adult students build their writing skills and their self-confidence.

Keep in mind these general tips for helping students improve their writing skills:
- Provide frequent uninterrupted times for writing.
- Let students choose topics that interest them.
- Allow more time for actual writing than for practicing writing skills.
- Carry out each writing assignment yourself, and share your writing with students.
- Talk about the writing process as students write.

The Writing Process

Accomplished writers don't simply get an idea, write it down, and produce a final piece. But inexperienced writers don't know that. They need to be taught that good writing usually involves a process that includes these stages:

1. **Prewriting:** Decide on a topic; generate and organize ideas.
2. **Drafting:** Get ideas down on paper in sentences and paragraphs.
3. **Revising:** Clarify, expand, and refine the content.
4. **Editing:** Correct errors in grammar and mechanics.
5. **Recopying:** Write a final draft, and share it with others.

To begin a discussion of the writing process, ask students to describe what they do when they write. As they describe their processes, name the stages for them:

Student: "First I write the whole thing all at once. Then my wife checks my spelling and punctuation for me."

Instructor: "Your first step is called writing a draft. When your wife checks for errors, she is editing your work. Both of these steps are stages in the writing process."

Show students the summary of the writing process in the Reference Handbook in the back of their books. Briefly explain the stages. Do one or both of the following:
- Use a piece of your own writing to illustrate the stages. Show students your first draft, explain how you revised and edited the piece, and show them your final draft.

- Work with students as they do the writing section of each lesson. Help them choose topics and brainstorm ideas about them. Model ways they can plan what to write before they write a draft. During the Writing Process section of each unit review, help students revise, edit, and recopy the draft they choose.

When students are prewriting, help them use simple outlines, lists, or graphic organizers to organize their thoughts. Several PCMs in this book can be used to help students generate and organize ideas.

Each time students begin a piece of sustained writing, encourage them to refer to the Reference Handbook in their student book.

Journals

Keeping a journal will help students become comfortable with the flow of writing. Encourage students to write their thoughts, activities, or whatever they would like in a daily or weekly journal. Emphasize that journals don't need to be revised or edited.

- **A personal journal** includes a student's thoughts, feelings, or observations on anything of interest. Students can keep these journals private or share them if they choose to.
- **A dialogue journal** is a written dialogue between you and the student. The student shares thoughts, feelings, and observations. You read what the student has written and write responses. You should not correct the student's writing. You may, however, model corrections in your responses. For example, if the student has misspelled a word, you can use the correctly spelled word in your response.

Writing Portfolios

Writing portfolios document the variety of writing your students do, and they provide an effective way for you to review and evaluate a student's work. More important, they let students see their own progress over time. Seeing progress is one of the most important factors in developing confidence in their writing. In addition, writing portfolios can demonstrate a student's

- ability to communicate
- use of the writing process
- scope of writing
- mastery of specific tasks

To make a writing portfolio, have students date all their writings and keep them in a working folder. Review these writings together periodically, and discuss areas of improvement. Students can select special pieces to place in a writing portfolio or in a more comprehensive progress portfolio. Here are some tips for developing either type of portfolio:

- If a student takes a piece of work through the writing process, staple the drafts together with the final product on top. Date all drafts.
- Have students use PCM 10: Tips for Preparing a Progress Portfolio to select pieces from their working folders to include in their portfolio. Have them explain why they chose those pieces.
- Use PCM 11: Portfolio Conference Questionnaire to help students evaluate their progress.

About Spelling

Students need to understand that while spelling is important in effective writing, becoming a good speller is a long-term process. They need not correct every spelling error in every piece. Take a long-term approach by following these suggestions:

- Have students keep a personal spelling list. They can label each page of a notebook with a letter of the alphabet. They should write words they want to know how to spell on the appropriate pages. They might also include a sentence for each target word.
- Base spelling assignments on words that students want or need to know. Make lists of words that students commonly use and misspell.
- Look for patterns in students' errors, and teach rules that relate to the most common mistakes.

Voyager 4 Teacher's Notes

Pre-Assessment

Before you begin Unit 1 with students, have them complete the Student Self-Assessment and the Skills Preview at the beginning of *Voyager 4* (see Using the Student Self-Assessments, page 15, and Using the Skills Preview, page 15).

In addition to *Voyager 4,* students will need
- folders in which to keep their finished work and their work in progress (see Working Folders, page 7)
- a spiral-bound or three-ring notebook to use as a personal dictionary (see Personal Dictionaries, page 18)
- a spiral-bound or three-ring notebook to use as a personal spelling list (see page 20)

▶ Unit 1: Staying Healthy

Part of Unit	Voyager 4 pages	TRG pages	Workbook pages
Overview	13	21 – 22	
Lesson 1	14 – 23	22 – 24	4 – 5
Lesson 2	24 – 31	24 – 25	6
Lesson 3	32 – 41	25 – 26	7 – 8
Writing Skills Mini-Lesson	42	26	9
Unit 1 Review	43 – 44	26	10 – 13

Student Objectives

Reading
- Read a story, a pamphlet, and an article.
- Apply the reading strategies of using prior experience, setting a purpose, and predicting content.
- Recognize problems and solutions, apply information, and understand cause and effect.

Writing
- Write a paragraph, fill in a KWL chart, and create a chart.

Speaking and Listening
- Retell, discuss, and ask questions.

Life Skill
- Read medicine labels, read a food chart, and fill in a medical history form.

▶ Unit 1 PCMs
PCM 1: KWHL Chart
PCM 4: Problem/Solution Work Sheet
PCM 5: Cause-and-Effect Chart
PCM 8: Strategies for Recognizing Words
PCM 9: Student Progress Tracking Sheet

▶ Personal Dictionaries and Spelling Lists
Encourage students to add words they would like to learn to their dictionaries and spelling lists during each lesson in Unit 1.

▶ Word Recognition Strategies
If students need practice with recognizing words, distribute copies of PCM 8 for them to work with.

Unit 1 Overview (p. 13)

The overview introduces the theme "Staying Healthy" and encourages students to relate to it personally before they begin Lesson 1. Call attention to the art, and discuss how it relates to the theme. Read the overview to students, or ask for volunteers to read it aloud. Discuss students' answers to the questions.

Be an Active Reader Explain that experienced readers are active readers—they think about the information they are reading and try to figure out words or ideas they don't understand. Encourage students to mark things they don't understand with question marks and underline any words they don't know. Tell them they will return to any marks they make after they have finished the entire selection.

Note: Some scientific and medical terms in Unit 1 may not be included in students' dictionaries. Be prepared to pronounce them for students and offer a brief definition when appropriate.

Lesson 1 (p. 14)

Learning Goals Discuss the learning goals. Explain that Lesson 1 will focus on these goals.

Before You Read Point out that students will apply the strategy of using their prior experience as they read the story in this lesson. Explain that experienced readers use their own experience to help them understand what they read.

Read the paragraph and the checklist. Encourage students to check off any health tip they have used. Explain that their knowledge of such tips may help them to relate to the main character in the story.

Preview the Reading Read the text, and demonstrate to students how to preview a reading. Point out the title. Point out the illustrations, asking pertinent questions such as "What seems to be happening in this picture?" and "How does the character appear to be feeling?" Encourage students to imagine what changes Pat will consider.

Use the Strategy In Before You Read, students began working with a reading strategy. Use the Strategy encourages students to continue to apply this strategy as they read. One or more Check-ins within the reading selection also remind students to apply the strategy as they read. Discuss the questions. Tell students to try to follow the directions as they read the selection.

"I've Got to Change" Have students read the story silently. Be sure students use the Check-ins to help them apply the strategy of using their experience to better understand the reading. Encourage students to mark the text as explained in Be an Active Reader on page 13 in *Voyager 4*.

You may want to assign volunteers the roles of Pat and the other characters—including a narrator—to read aloud.

At the end of the selection, have students reread sections they marked to see if they can understand those sections now. If not, have them discuss the sections with a partner or with you. If students are unable to figure out the words they underlined, have them use PCM 8. If they still have trouble with words, encourage them to use a dictionary.

If students need help using a dictionary, demonstrate how. Then give them practice in looking up words, using the pronunciation guide, and determining which definition applies.

"Laughter Is Good Medicine" Explain that cartoons often deal with serious issues—in this case, dieting. Ask students to read the cartoon silently. Then ask for a volunteer to read it aloud. Ask if students can relate to Charlie Brown or Snoopy. Discuss why Snoopy throws his dish at Charlie Brown. Finally, discuss why we enjoy cartoons about serious issues—because it's easier to look at such matters if we approach them with humor.

After You Read

A. Have students answer questions 1–4 independently and check their answers in the Answer Key. Discuss their answers. To improve reading comprehension skills, have students find evidence for the correct answers in the selection.

   For question 5, explain that students should tell the events in the story in their own words, in the order in which they occurred. Suggest they start retelling by saying, "'I've Got to Change' is about . . ."

B. Have students look at the list in Before You Read to get started. Ask them to list three to five more tips and share them with the class.

C. Have students discuss the questions in pairs or small groups. Encourage them to consider their own experience and the experiences of friends and family as they answer the questions. Ask volunteers to share their answers with the entire group. If students answer the questions in writing, encourage them to write in a personal or a dialogue journal. (See Working with Adult Student Writers, page 19.)

Extending the Reading Ask students to discuss some common health concerns. Encourage them to use a phone book or newspaper to find possible sources of help for various health problems. Then have them share this information with the class.

Think About It: Recognize Problems and Solutions
On the board, write the headings *Problem, Cause,* and *Solution.* Use a simple example to introduce the concept of recognizing problems and solutions (e.g., *"Dominic often overslept and was late for work. He was in danger of losing his job. Dominic realized the cause of his problem—he stayed up too late. So he went to bed earlier and stopped oversleeping. Now he gets to work on time."*). Ask students to identify problem, cause, and solution in the example. List them under the correct headings.

Read the introductory paragraphs as students follow along. Mention that students recognize problems and solutions in their own lives every day, and that they can apply this skill to help them understand many things they read as well.
  A. Read this section aloud. Ask students to write answers to the questions independently. Then read the final paragraph. Ask, *"Were your answers similar to the explanation here?"*
  B. Explain that students will identify the components of Pat's solution in this Practice. Work through question 1 with students. Let them do questions 2–4 on their own.

Talk About It Have students complete the chart on their own; then have them discuss their answers with a partner. Have students discuss whether their eating habits are healthful or not and why.

Extending the Skill Use PCM 4. Ask students to write down a problem they or someone they know has. Have them identify the cause or causes and a possible solution. As an example, repeat the scenario about Dominic in Think About It above, or summarize the central problem and solution in "I've Got to Change." Next, have students work in pairs to read each other's problem, cause, and solution. Then ask students to brainstorm other possible solutions to each problem. Finally, have students evaluate the solutions and choose the best one. Have them date their work sheets and put them in their working folders.

More Practice *Voyager 4 Workbook* p. 4. The workbook exercises are designed to be done independently. They should not require teacher input.

Write About It: Write a Paragraph About Pat Read the first two paragraphs aloud. Point out examples of paragraphs in students' books and in other materials. Explain that three common methods can indicate a paragraph: indenting the first line, double spacing between paragraphs, or both.

Be sure students understand that all sentences in a paragraph relate to the same main idea. Remind students that the main idea is the main point that a writer wants to make. Explain that while many paragraphs contain a topic sentence, many others do not—the main idea is expressed over the course of the entire paragraph. This is particularly true of narratives like "I've Got to Change."
  A. Read the directions. Ask students to write the remaining details themselves.
  B. Read the directions. Encourage students to write paragraphs on their own. If necessary, help reluctant writers with the first detail sentence. Next, have volunteers read their paragraphs. Discuss how the details give information about the main idea, which is summed up in the topic sentence. Have students date their writing and put it in their working folders.

Life Skill: Read Medicine Labels Read the first paragraph. Discuss the importance of reading medicine labels correctly.

Have students pair off to define the three vocabulary words. Check their definitions.

Read the list of guidelines, or ask students to take turns reading it aloud. Ask students to offer other guidelines they may know. Discuss the dangers of failing to follow any of the guidelines.

Practice Provide empty nonprescription or prescription pill bottles, or ask students to bring some to class. Have students read the labels. If the labels contain unfamiliar or hard-to-decode words, help students find them in a dictionary. Stress the importance of knowing all the information about any medicine they take.

Progress Evaluation Have students fill in copies of PCM 9 to include in their working folders.

Lesson 2 (p. 24)

Learning Goals Discuss the learning goals. Explain that Lesson 2 will focus on these goals.

Before You Read Point out that students will practice the strategy of setting a purpose as they read the chart and pamphlet in this lesson. Explain that experienced readers read for a purpose and have questions in mind before they begin to read.

Read the paragraph. Encourage students to write a few questions about the nutritional benefits of fruits and vegetables. Explain that they can look for the answers to their questions as they read.

Preview the Reading Have students read the directions and preview the selection. List on the board the kinds of information they expect to learn.

Use the Strategy See Lesson 1 notes.

"Eat More Fruits & Vegetables" Explain that pamphlets are written for a specific purpose, often to highlight important information about a topic. By scanning the section headings in the pamphlet, students can quickly get an idea of the information in the pamphlet. Explain how to use the footnotes to learn definitions of selected words.

Have students read the selection silently. Be sure students use the Check-ins to help them apply the strategy of setting a purpose. Encourage students to mark the text, as active readers do. At the end of the selection, have students check any questions they had to make sure they understand the text now. Encourage students to add any words they want to learn to their personal dictionaries.

After You Read
A. Follow the approach for questions 1–4 in Lesson 1.
B. Have students review the pamphlet as they answer the questions.

C. See Lesson 1 notes.

Extending the Reading Provide or ask students to bring charts and pamphlets on food and nutrition from local grocery stores or health clinics. Have students work in pairs to read the charts and pamphlets, noting what they already knew about the topic and what new facts they learned.

Think About It: Apply Information Read the introductory paragraph. Ask students to think about information they have read and how they have applied it to their own lives (e.g., studying the rules of the road when they learned to drive or following recipe directions step by step). List their responses on the board.
A. Read this section aloud. Ask students to use the chart to answer the question independently. Then have them share their responses.
B. Have students do the Practice for homework. During the next class, ask students to discuss which fruits and vegetables they currently eat and which they have tried for the first time.

Extending the Skill Have students share favorite recipes containing fruits or vegetables. Encourage students to try a new recipe at home. Discuss which recipes students like best and why.

More Practice *Voyager 4 Workbook* p. 6

Write About It: Fill In a KWL Chart Read the first paragraph. After students understand what a KWL chart is for, have them copy the headings on separate paper or provide them with copies of PCM 1. If you use PCM 1, tell them that they can write, "Read the article 'On the Go with Good Food'" in the *H* column, "How I Will Learn It."
A. Before students read the article, discuss what good foods they know they can eat if they are on the go. Point out that by filling in this chart, they are setting a purpose for reading the article and applying the strategy they used earlier.
B. Have students complete the last column on the KWL chart. Ask them to share with a partner or with the entire class what they have learned from the article. Have students date their charts and put them in their working folders.

Life Skill: A Closer Look at a Food Chart Read the first paragraph. Discuss with students the elements in a chart.

Have students read the second paragraph and then skim the chart to answer the question. Be sure they have read the chart correctly.

Practice Have students read the chart and answer the questions independently.

Progress Evaluation Have students fill in copies of PCM 9 to include in their working folders.

Lesson 3 (p. 32)

Learning Goals Discuss the learning goals. Explain that Lesson 3 will focus on these goals.

Before You Read Point out that students will practice the strategy of predicting content as they read the article in this lesson. Explain that trying to predict what information an article will include can help them understand what they read.

Read the paragraph. Encourage students to write down a few kinds of information they think they might read in the selection.

Preview the Reading Have students read the directions and preview the selection. List their predictions on the board.

Use the Strategy See Lesson 1 notes.

"How to Avoid Food That Makes You Sick" Have students read the selection silently. Be sure students use the Check-ins to help them apply the strategy of predicting. Help with the pronunciations of scientific terms, if necessary. Encourage students to mark the text, as active readers do. At the end of the selection, have students check any marks they have made.

After You Read
A. Follow the approach for questions 1–4 in Lesson 1.
B. Have students compare the predictions they made with what they found in the article. You may also want to mention other techniques used to keep food safe, such as irradiation.

C. See Lesson 1 notes.

Extending the Reading Provide samples of safe-handling directions from packages of meat, fish, or poultry bought from a store. Ask volunteers to read the directions and discuss them.

Think About It: Understand Cause and Effect Read the introductory paragraph. Ask students to give examples of cause and effect from their own experience.
A. Point out the use of cue words often found in cause-and-effect statements.

Write the headings *Cause, Cue words,* and *Effect* on the board. Work through the three examples with students, listing the correct information from each example under the appropriate heading. Be sure they understand that a statement sometimes mentions the effect before the cause (as in the third example).

B. Work through the first statement with students. Have them complete 2–7 on their own.

Talk About It Allow students to share their questions. Compile a class list.

Extending the Skill Use PCM 5. Provide or have students bring to class newspaper articles about nutrition and food-related topics. Have students work in pairs to look for cause-and-effect relationships and note them in the boxes on their copies of the PCM. Tell them also to note any cue words they find. Have students date their papers and put them in their working folders.

More Practice *Voyager 4 Workbook* p. 7

Write About It: Create a Chart Read and discuss the first paragraph. Then read the assignment.
A. Discuss the elements in the sample chart before students create their own charts. Have volunteers suggest means of proper storage, preparation tips, and internal cooking temperature before they begin to write.
B. Help students create their own charts. You may want to suggest or have on hand other sources of information to fill in the chart. Have students date their charts and put them in their working folders.

Life Skill: Fill In a Medical History Form Read the introductory paragraph. Point out how important it is to put the correct information on a medical history form. Discuss what might happen if incorrect or inaccurate information is given.

Read the form with students. Interpret any unfamiliar terminology. Discuss the most common allergies that people have. List on the board illnesses students have had other than the ones listed on the form.

Practice Have students complete the form. Tell them they have the option of making up information rather than listing personal information, if they prefer.

Progress Evaluation Have students fill in copies of PCM 9 to include in their working folders.

Writing Skills Mini-Lesson: Fixing Sentence Fragments (p. 42)

Read and discuss the first paragraph. You might want to have students identify some of the subjects and verbs in the paragraph.

1. Read and discuss the first example. Point out why the fragment is not a sentence. By adding a verb and other words, you can make the fragment into a complete sentence. Ask students for other examples of fragments and how the fragments can be fixed by adding a verb and/or other words.

2. Read and discuss the second example. Explain that a dependent clause begins with a connecting word, such as *if,* and cannot stand alone. Ask students for other dependent clauses, and have them suggest how the clauses can be made into complete sentences.

Practice If students are having trouble identifying fragments and complete sentences, go over the paragraph with them, underlining fragments that need to be fixed. Then have students complete the exercise independently.

More Practice *Voyager 4 Workbook* pp. 9 and 13

Unit 1 Review (p. 43)

Explain that this review will help students evaluate what they have learned in Unit 1. Give students plenty of time to complete the review.

Reading Review Have students read the story and complete the questions independently.

Writing Process Before students begin the Writing Process, have them turn to page 160 in the student book. Discuss the five steps of the writing process. Explain that students have already completed steps 1 and 2 for the two pieces they wrote in Unit 1. Help students locate the draft they would like to work with further. Work with students as they revise, edit, and create a final draft.

To help students with revising, go over the questions at the bottom of page 44 in the student book. When they get to the editing stage, remind students to locate and fix any fragments, making sure all of their sentences are complete. Have students date their writing and put it in their working folders.

More Practice *Voyager 4 Workbook* p. 10

Extending the Theme To extend the theme "Staying Healthy," explore with students the benefits of exercise. Have them complete the first two columns of PCM 1. Ask them to bring in articles, brochures, or books to help them learn what they want to know. Then have them fill in the third column of the PCM. Students can work in pairs or groups to help each other locate information. Then have students complete the last column of their charts.

Final Note Review with students the copies of PCM 9 that they placed in their working folders. Ask what additional help they think they need with material from the three lessons and the Writing Skills Mini-Lesson in Unit 1. Discuss possible ways of meeting those needs.

▶ Unit 2: Get That Job!

Part of Unit	Voyager 4 pages	TRG pages	Workbook pages
Overview	45	27	
Lesson 4	46 – 55	27 – 28	14 – 15
Lesson 5	56 – 63	28 – 29	16
Lesson 6	64 – 73	29 – 30	17 – 18
Writing Skills Mini-Lesson	74	31	19
Unit 2 Review	75 – 76	31	20 – 23

Student Objectives

Reading
- Read a story, a job application, and an article.
- Apply the reading strategies of visualizing, predicting features, and using prior knowledge.
- Understand cause and effect, locate key facts, and identify the main idea.

Writing
- Write about a dream job, fill in a personal information sheet, and write about an interesting job.

Speaking and Listening
- Retell, discuss, and role-play.

Life Skill
- Interpret want ads, fill in a job application, and fill in a job network web.

▶ Unit 2 PCMs
PCM 1: KWHL Chart
PCM 2: Main Idea and Details Organizer
PCM 5: Cause-and-Effect Chart
PCM 8: Strategies for Recognizing Words
PCM 9: Student Progress Tracking Sheet

▶ Personal Dictionaries and Spelling Lists
Encourage students to add words they would like to learn to their dictionaries and spelling lists during each lesson in Unit 2.

▶ Word Recognition Strategies
If students need practice with recognizing words, distribute copies of PCM 8 for them to work with.

See **Lesson 1 notes** for lesson segments not addressed in these notes.

Unit 2 Overview (p. 45)

The overview introduces the theme "Get That Job!" and encourages students to relate to it before they begin the unit. Call attention to the art, and discuss how it relates to the unit theme. Read the overview to students, or ask volunteers to read it.

Be an Active Reader See Unit 1 notes.

Lesson 4 (p. 46)

Learning Goals Discuss the learning goals.

Before You Read Read the first paragraph aloud. Point out that students will practice the strategy of visualizing to better understand "Easy Job, Good Wages." Explain that experienced readers visualize, or picture in their minds, what they read.

Read the pre-reading activity aloud. Encourage students to visualize easy and difficult jobs, and ask volunteers to describe what they visualize.

Preview the Reading Have students read the directions and preview the selection. Have them share what they imagine they will find in some of the paragraphs.

"Easy Job, Good Wages" Have students read the story silently. Be sure students use the Check-ins to help them apply the strategy of visualizing. Encourage students to mark the text, as active readers do. At the end of the selection, have students check any marks they have made.

Have volunteers read the story aloud. Discuss how picturing what is happening to the character helps students identify with him more fully.

After You Read

B. Have students recall the mental pictures they formed as they read the story and suggest different ways the job could have been done. Compile a class list of suggestions.

Extending the Reading Have students work in small groups. Have each group choose a different job to think about. Have them create a list of questions that a job seeker might ask an employer about the job they chose. Discuss the various lists.

Think About It: Understand Cause and Effect

Review with students the concept of cause and effect. Ask if they can suggest a few everyday examples. Write each example with the cause stated before the effect (e.g., "Soo Young's car wouldn't start, so she was late for her appointment") and then with the effect stated before the cause (e.g., "Soo Young was late for her appointment because her car wouldn't start").

A. Read as students follow along. Ask students to answer the question. Discuss their responses.

B. Work through the first passage in the Practice. Help students identify the cause and the effect correctly. Have students do 2–5 on their own.

Talk About It Suggest students jot down a short sequence of events or time line to help them remember the story. Remind students to include all the details they visualized as they read the story the first time. Students might also consider why both brothers responded to the same want ad and what they learned from their experience.

Extending the Skill Use PCM 5. Provide a newspaper or magazine article that contains several cause-and-effect relationships. Try to find one on a job- or economy-related topic. Have students work with a partner or small group to identify causes and effects and to fill in PCM 5. Have students date their charts and put them in their working folders.

More Practice *Voyager 4 Workbook* p. 14

Write About It: Write About Your Dream Job Read the first paragraph aloud. Ask students to picture the type of job that they would like and that would best use their skills and abilities. List volunteers' responses on the board.

Review with students the concepts of main idea, topic sentence, and details. Read "My Dream Job" aloud, pointing out the topic sentence that states the main idea at the beginning of the paragraph. Work with students to identify the supporting details in the other sentences. Give students copies of PCM 2 to help them identify the details and see the relationships between them and the main idea.

Be sure students answer the questions and fill in the details about their dream job before they write their paragraphs. Remind students to begin their descriptions with a topic sentence and to use their information sheet to complete their paragraphs. Ask volunteers to share their completed paragraphs with the class. Have students date their writing and put it in their working folders.

Life Skill: Interpret Want Ads Read the introductory paragraph. Discuss how important it is for students to know how to read want ads when they are looking for a job.

Ask students to take turns spelling aloud the abbreviations and reading the words they stand for. Ask if they know other help-wanted abbreviations. If so, list the abbreviations on the board. Have students work independently to read the sample want ad and interpret the abbreviations. Discuss their answers.

Practice Have students do the exercise independently or with a partner.

Extending the Life Skill Distribute copies of newspaper want ads. Have students find the abbreviations in each want ad and tell what they mean. Encourage students to develop a glossary of want ad abbreviations to add to their personal dictionaries.

Progress Evaluation Have students fill in copies of PCM 9 to include in their working folders.

Lesson 5 (p. 56)

Learning Goals Discuss the learning goals.

Before You Read Tell students that they will practice the strategy of predicting features as they read the job application. Explain that this will help students be better prepared to answer the questions on such a form.

Read the first paragraph and pre-reading activity aloud. Ask students to check off those questions they think will be asked on a job application.

Preview the Reading Have students read the directions and preview the selection. List the different kinds of information on the board. Ask a volunteer to respond to the second question.

"Determined to Find a Job" Have students read the scenario, the tips, and the filled-in job application form silently. Encourage them to mark the text, as active readers do. When they finish reading, have them check any marks they have made.

After You Read

B. Have students check their predictions with the actual questions on the form before they answer the question. Make sure students understand that employers cannot legally ask about an applicant's age, marital status, race, religion, or national origin except when the job qualifications require the information.

Extending the Reading Discuss the types of questions the grocery store manager would ask Kim during a job interview. Then have pairs of students role-play the job interview. If there is time, have pairs reverse roles so that students have a chance to play both interviewer and applicant. Discuss students' reactions.

Think About It: Locate Key Facts Read and discuss the introductory paragraphs. Ask students to locate the section headings *Education* and *Previous Employment* on the application form in the lesson.
A. Read this section aloud. Make sure students know the distinction between education and training, and between certificates and licenses. Discuss how the term *skills* is used in this section. List students' suggestions of various job skills on the board.
B. Have students do the Practice independently. Discuss their work.

Talk About It Encourage students to review Kim's responses on her job application and use them as a basis for their decision. Have them give specific reasons they would or would not hire Kim.

Extending the Skill Bring in or ask students to get application forms from local businesses, such as grocery stores, restaurants, hardware stores, libraries, and manufacturing companies. Then have students compare the kind of information they are expected to fill in on each form.

More Practice *Voyager 4 Workbook* p. 16

Write About It: Fill In a Personal Information Sheet Read the first paragraph aloud. Discuss each of the form's components and how important it is to know this information when looking for a job. After they complete the form, students may want to prepare a similar information sheet to take home.

Life Skill: Fill In a Job Application Form Refer students to the tips on how to fill in a job application form on page 57 in the student book. Have them read through the form to see if they understand what kind of information is being asked under each section heading. Explain that much of the data on their personal information sheet can be used to complete the job application form. Make sure students understand the final paragraph about authorization to contact references, and the fact that lying on a job application form can lead to being fired from a job. Tell students to print neatly or write legibly to complete the application form.

Progress Evaluation Have students fill in copies of PCM 9 to include in their working folders.

Lesson 6 (p. 64)

Learning Goals Discuss the learning goals.

Before You Read Point out that students will practice the strategy of using their prior knowledge as they read the article in this lesson. Remind them that thinking about what they already know about a topic before they begin to read helps them to better understand what they read.

Read and discuss the pre-reading activity. Have students write down ideas they would include in an article about job hunting and then share them with the class.

Preview the Reading Have students read the directions and preview the selection. Ask if any of the students' ideas noted in Before You Read have been included.

"Tips for Job Hunting" Have students read the selection silently. Be sure students stop for the Check-ins to help them apply the strategy of using their prior knowledge as they read the article. Encourage students to mark the text, as active readers do. At the end of the selection, have students check any marks they have made. Discuss how the frequent headings, bulleted list, and diagram help show how the information is organized.

After You Read
B. Have students form pairs or small groups to discuss the additional tips about job hunting. Also have them share and discuss any information they noted in Before You Read that was not mentioned in the article.

Extending the Reading Encourage students to think carefully and to list the skills and abilities they have that could help them get and keep a job. Remind them that skills used by homemakers and volunteers—such as organizational or money-handling skills—can be valuable to an employer. Have them note what kinds of jobs they have had and what kinds they are interested in. Help them consider other jobs that match their skills and abilities. Have students date their lists and put them in their working folders.

Think About It: Identify the Main Idea Read and discuss the introductory paragraph.
A. Read the first paragraph. Ask a volunteer to read the first section of the article aloud. Discuss how the suggested main idea is the most important point of the section. Have a volunteer read the section "Brush Up Your Skills" and suggest how to sum up its main point.

B. Have students work with a partner or small group to complete the Practice.

Talk About It Before role-playing, partners should decide on the type of company they are interested in. Have pairs make up a list of questions an interviewer would ask a job applicant, such as "Why do you want to work for this company?" and "What skills and abilities do you bring to this job?"

Extending the Skill Find an article with a clear main idea and details, preferably related to job-seeking. Have students read the article and use PCM 2 to identify the main idea and details. If the article is divided into sections, each with its own main idea, provide a suitable number of copies of PCM 2. Have students date their papers and put them in their working folders.

More Practice *Voyager 4 Workbook* p. 17

Write About It: Write About an Interesting Job
Read and discuss the introduction. Have the group generate on the board a list of possible jobs to help students choose a job to research.
A. Review the meaning of each heading on the KWHL chart before students begin the activity.
B. Remind students to include in their paragraphs a topic sentence and the key details from the *K* and *L* columns of their KWHL charts. Students may want to compile this valuable job information into a resource they all can refer to (see Extending the Theme). Have students date their charts and place them in their working folders.

Life Skill: Fill In a Job Network Web Read and discuss the first three paragraphs. Have students refer to the web on page 67 to see how extensive a job network web can be.

Practice Help students complete a job network web of their own. Be sure they list the names of individuals who may help them—not merely groups such as friends. Have students date their webs and place them in their working folders.

Progress Evaluation Have students fill in copies of PCM 9 to include in their working folders.

Writing Skills Mini-Lesson: Fixing Run-on Sentences (p. 74)

Read and discuss the introductory paragraph.

1. Read and discuss the first way to fix a run-on sentence, along with the example. Ask students to suggest another example of a run-on, or suggest one, such as "Things cost more my pay has stayed the same." Write the run-on on the board, and ask a volunteer to fix it.

2–3. Follow the procedure described for 1. Use the same example.

Practice When you are sure students understand how to fix run-on sentences, have them complete the Practice independently. Have students date their work and put it in their working folders.

More Practice *Voyager 4 Workbook* pp. 19 and 23

Unit 2 Review (p. 75)

Follow the process described in Unit 1. When students get to the editing stage in the writing process, remind them to look for and fix any sentence fragments and run-on sentences.

More Practice *Voyager 4 Workbook* p. 20

Extending the Theme Use PCM 1. Ask each student to research a job that will be in demand in the next 10 years. Have students fill in the chart before and after they read, including how they found the information. Keep the charts in a job file for all class members to share, or compile the charts into a class chart or list to display.

Final Note Review with students the copies of PCM 9 that they completed for this unit. Ask what additional help they think they need with material from the three lessons and the Writing Skills Mini-Lesson in Unit 2. Discuss possible ways of meeting those needs.

▶ Unit 3: A Sense of Community

Part of Unit	Voyager 4 pages	TRG pages	Workbook pages
Overview	77	32	
Lesson 7	78 – 87	32 – 33	24 – 25
Lesson 8	88 – 95	33 – 34	26
Lesson 9	96 – 105	34 – 35	27 – 28
Writing Skills Mini-Lesson	106	35 – 36	29
Unit 3 Review	107 – 108	36	30 – 33

Student Objectives

Reading
- Read an article, a scenario and map with key, and a brochure.
- Apply the reading strategies of using prior experience, predicting features, and predicting content.
- Recognize problems and solutions, follow directions, and locate key facts.

Writing
- Write about a problem and a solution, write directions, and write an announcement.

Speaking and Listening
- Discuss, ask for and give directions, and use telephone skills.

Life Skill
- Use a phone book, draw a map, and use the library.

▶ Unit 3 PCMs
PCM 4: Problem/Solution Work Sheet
PCM 8: Strategies for Recognizing Words
PCM 9: Student Progress Tracking Sheet

▶ Personal Dictionaries and Spelling Lists
Encourage students to add words they would like to learn to their dictionaries and spelling lists during each lesson in Unit 3.

▶ Word Recognition Strategies
If students need work on recognizing words, distribute copies of PCM 8 for them to use.

See Lesson 1 notes for lesson segments not addressed in these notes.

Unit 3 Overview (p. 77)

The overview introduces the theme "A Sense of Community" and encourages students to relate to it personally before they begin the unit. Call attention to the art, and discuss how it relates to the unit theme. Have volunteers read the overview and discuss it.

Be an Active Reader See Unit 1 notes.

Lesson 7 (p. 78)

Learning Goals Discuss the learning goals.

Before You Read Point out that students will use the strategy of using prior experience as they read the article in this lesson.

Read the first paragraph. Ask volunteers to share some of the problems they experienced as teenagers. Then have students write and share their own opinions about how to help teens in their community. You may have them work in groups and brainstorm to get ideas.

Preview the Reading Have students read the directions and preview the selection. Also ask students to look closely at the art. Discuss what students think the title refers to.

"Make Sure What You're Looking at Is What You Really See" Have students read the article silently. Be sure they use the Check-ins to help them apply the strategy of using prior experience. Encourage students to mark the text, as active readers do. At the end of the selection, have students check any marks they have made. You may want volunteers to take turns reading it aloud, after noting the informal language and conversational sentence structure used.

"Do Teenagers Need Help?" Have students read the first two paragraphs. Demonstrate how to read the graph as you read the third paragraph. Then ask students to answer the questions about the graph.

After You Read
B. Have students pair off or form small groups to compare their experiences and discuss their responses.

Extending the Reading Bring to class an almanac with statistics on teen drug use or unemployment. Help students read and interpret the figures. Then have pairs use statistics from the almanac to create their own graphs.

Think About It: Recognize Problems and Solutions
Read with students the steps needed to solve a problem. For an example of each step, expand on the problem/solution example used in Lesson 1: Dominic constantly overslept and was late for work (problem). He stayed up too late (cause). He could buy a loud alarm clock (solution) or go to bed earlier (solution). He decided to go to bed earlier. He stopped oversleeping and now gets to work on time.

A. Discuss the example. Read the excerpts from the article that identify steps 1, 2, and 3 (the problem, cause, and solution).

B. Have students work in pairs or small groups to fill in the problem/solution work sheet.

Talk About It After students have discussed the teen crime problem in their community, have small groups use PCM 4 to analyze the problem and consider solutions for it.

Extending the Skill Use PCM 4. Ask students to think about a problem they have on the job, at home, or in class. Have students work independently to complete a problem/solution work sheet for their problem. Have students date their work sheets and put them in their working folders.

More Practice *Voyager 4 Workbook* p. 24

Write About It: Write About a Problem and a Solution Read the first paragraph aloud.

A. Have students choose one of the suggested topics or think of one of their own. Ask them to think carefully about the causes of the problem and possible solutions and then fill in the problem/solution work sheet on their own.

B. Be sure students understand the structure of the three-paragraph essay they are to write. Have students date their writing and put it in their working folders.

Life Skill: Use a Phone Book Read the introductory paragraphs aloud. Discuss how important it is to know how to find resources in the community—both emergency and nonemergency services.

Work through the three questions about the phone book sample as a class. Ask volunteers to explain their answers.

Provide phone books so students can complete the second activity in pairs. Or if students have phone books at home, have them find the numbers of the various agencies and services and compare their answers in class.

Note: The names of these agencies and services vary from place to place. They also are found in different sections of different phone books. Be sure to locate these numbers in your local phone book first, so you can help students find them.

Practice Have students complete the exercise on their own. Ask volunteers to share their findings with the class.

Progress Evaluation Have students fill in copies of PCM 9 to include in their working folders.

Lesson 8 (p. 88)

Learning Goals Discuss the learning goals.

Before You Read Read the introductory paragraph and the pre-reading activity. Encourage students to think about parks they have been in and then list things Juan and his children might see in their visit to a park.

Preview the Reading Have students read the directions and preview the selection.

"Let's Go Out!" Have students read the selection silently. Be sure they read the Check-in. Ask volunteers to locate the 10 places on the map.

After You Read
B. Have students check their predictions to see if they matched what is found on Boston Common. Discuss their responses to the questions.

Extending the Reading Provide city or area maps, or ask students to bring in maps with keys. Have students work in pairs to write a list of questions about places and distances on their map (e.g., "What direction is city A from city B?" "How many blocks is A Street from B Street?" etc.). Have pairs exchange maps and answer the questions.

Think About It: Follow Directions Read the introductory paragraph. Discuss the clue words that make directions easier to understand and follow.

A. Work through the first example to make sure students understand how to read the key on the map.

Ask students to follow the next set of directions on the Boston Common map. Check to see if they arrive at the correct location.

B. Have students complete the Practice independently. Have them check their answers in the Answer Key.

Talk About It Make sure students start their directions from a clear, recognizable location—perhaps the site of their class. They should also specify whether they are giving directions for walking, driving, or riding on public transportation.

Extending the Skill Use the maps used previously in Extending the Reading. Have students work in pairs to write sets of directions. Have them exchange maps and directions with other pairs. Have pairs follow the directions to figure out the destination. Have students date their directions and put them in their working folders.

More Practice *Voyager 4 Workbook* p. 26

Write About It: Write Directions Read the first paragraph. As always, students' privacy should be respected. If a student does not wish to reveal his or her home address, substitute a public place as the destination.

A. If students are not sure of the names of streets, provide a local map or have them bring one.

B. Read through the tips with students. They may need additional paper to write their directions. Have students date their directions and put them in their working folders.

Life Skill: Draw a Map Read and discuss the explanatory paragraphs. Have students answer the questions and see if they have followed the directions correctly.

Practice Ask students to complete the activity on their own. Tell them to use the information from Write About It. Have students exchange maps with a partner to see if they have drawn and labeled the maps clearly and accurately. Have them date their work and put it in their working folders.

Progress Evaluation Have students fill in copies of PCM 9 to include in their working folders.

Lesson 9 (p. 96)

Learning Goals Discuss the learning goals.

Before You Read Point out that students will be using the strategy of predicting content. Read and discuss the introductory paragraph and pre-reading activity. Ask students to read the list and check all the services and materials they would expect to find in a library.

Preview the Reading Have students read the directions and preview the selection. Have volunteers answer the questions.

"Your Library: A Major Community Resource" Have students read the selection silently. Ask students to create their own Check-ins as they read by making an *X* in the margin next to each piece of information they predicted they would find. Encourage students to mark the text, as active readers do. At the end of the selection, have them check any marks they have made.

Explain that sometimes brochures use incomplete sentences. Identify some of the fragments on page 99. Have students tell the missing words (e.g., "Award-winning movies **are shown** every Friday at 8:00 P.M. Refreshments **are provided** courtesy of the Library Association."). Discuss the reasons (space and brevity) and whether leaving out words affects communicating the message. Then discuss the two announcements that follow the brochure.

After You Read

B. Have students check to see if their predictions matched the information in the brochure.

Extending the Reading Provide or ask students to bring in brochures from various places. Have students work in small groups to compare the brochures and list the elements that are common to them all.

Think About It: Locate Key Facts Read the introductory paragraph. Have students identify which of the *W* questions are being answered in the sample announcement. Explain that these items are the key facts in the announcement.

A. Ask students to read the announcement and underline the key facts they are asked to locate.

B. Read the directions for the Practice, and have students complete it independently.

Talk About It Have students work in pairs to brainstorm a list of questions they could ask a reference librarian. Each should then choose the question he or she is most interested in. If your library doesn't have a reference librarian, ask volunteers to call about the availability of specific titles or services.

Extending the Skill Demonstrate how to skim to locate key facts. Clues to look for while skimming include numbers; capital letters (which may signify names, places, and dates); and abbreviations such as *P.M.* Ask students to pick up a brochure from the local library or some other organization or business. Have them write a list of *who, what, when, where,* and *why* questions that are answered in the brochure. Then have students exchange their questions and brochure with a partner, who will answer the questions and locate the key facts in the brochure.

More Practice *Voyager 4 Workbook* p. 27

Write About It: Write an Announcement Read and discuss the introduction. Ask students to name the kinds of information they have seen in announcements on a community bulletin board.

A. Have students complete the list of *W* questions. If they have trouble choosing a topic for their announcement, suggest they pretend they want to sell something.

B. Ask volunteers to read the tips for writing an announcement. Have available the brochures that were used in the extension activities so that students can see more examples of design. You might want to provide colored paper. If a computer is available, help students choose special fonts to make their announcements attractive. Have them date their announcements and put them in their working folders.

Life Skill: Use the Library as a Community Resource Read and discuss the introductory paragraphs. Point out how useful it is for people to have a library card. If they do not have a driver's license or voter registration card, people can often bring mail sent to them (for instance, an electric bill or a phone bill) to prove their address.

Practice Have students complete the activity on their own.

Extending the Life Skill Encourage students who do not have a library card to obtain one.

Progress Evaluation Have students fill in copies of PCM 9 to include in their working folders.

Writing Skills Mini-Lesson: Correcting Usage Problems (p. 106)

Explain that usage problems are common errors people make in using English.

1. Work through the first rule with students. Ask students to think of other examples. Write them on the board.

2. Read the second rule and examples. Give an example of a comparison with *more* and *most* (*more useful, most useful*). Remind students that adding *-er* or *-est* to a word sometimes

involves a spelling change. Ask students to suggest other correct examples of comparison, and write them on the board.

3. Read the third rule and examples. Have students provide more examples of how these words are used correctly, and write them on the board.

Practice When students feel comfortable with these rules, have them find the errors in the paragraph and then write the paragraph correctly on separate paper. Have students date their writing and put it in their working folders.

More Practice *Voyager 4 Workbook* pp. 29 and 33

Unit 3 Review (p. 107)

Follow the process described in Unit 1. When students get to the editing stage in the writing process, remind them to find and fix any fragments, run-on sentences, and usage problems.

More Practice *Voyager 4 Workbook* p. 30

Extending the Theme To extend the theme "A Sense of Community," have students survey the yellow pages, the brochures, and other real-life reading materials they have used in this unit. Have students create a chart listing the types of services offered in their community.

Final Note Review with students the copies of PCM 9 that they have completed for this unit. Ask what additional help they think they need with material from the three lessons and the Writing Skills Mini-Lesson in Unit 3. Discuss possible ways of meeting those needs.

▶ Unit 4: Crime and the Law

Part of Unit	Voyager 4 pages	TRG pages	Workbook pages
Overview	109	37	
Lesson 10	110 – 119	37 – 38	34 – 35
Lesson 11	120 – 127	38 – 39	36
Lesson 12	128 – 137	39 – 40	37 – 38
Writing Skills Mini-Lesson	138	41	39
Unit 4 Review	139 – 140	41	40 – 43

Student Objectives

Reading

- Read an article, a political cartoon, letters to the editor, and a story.
- Apply the reading strategies of using prior knowledge, setting a purpose, and visualizing.
- Apply information, identify the main idea, and follow a sequence of events.

Writing

- Write an opinion, a letter to the editor, and a poem.

Speaking and Listening

- Answer questions, discuss, and retell.

Life Skill

- Read a bar graph, analyze a political cartoon, and read a parking ticket.

▶ Unit 4 PCMs

PCM 2: Main Idea and Details Organizer
PCM 7: Idea Map
PCM 8: Strategies for Recognizing Words
PCM 9: Student Progress Tracking Sheet

▶ Personal Dictionaries and Spelling Lists

Encourage students to add words they would like to learn to their dictionaries and spelling lists during each lesson in Unit 4.

▶ Word Recognition Strategies

If students need practice with recognizing words, distribute copies of PCM 8 for them to work with.

See Lesson 1 notes for lesson segments not addressed in these notes.

Unit 4 Overview (p. 109)

The overview introduces the theme "Crime and the Law" and encourages students to relate to it personally before they begin the unit. Call attention to the art, and discuss how it relates to the theme. Have volunteers read the overview and discuss it.

Be an Active Reader See Unit 1 notes.

Lesson 10 (p. 110)

Learning Goals Discuss the learning goals.

Before You Read Point out that students will practice the strategy of using their prior knowledge. Read the introductory paragraph aloud. Write the names of the three cases on the board: *Brown v. Board of Education, Gideon v. Wainright,* and *Miranda v. Arizona.* Explain that *v.* means *versus,* or *against.* Ask what students may know about any of the cases. Work through the pre-reading vocabulary activity orally.

Preview the Reading Have students read the directions and preview the selection. Ask volunteers what predictions they made, and list those predictions on the board.

"Three 'Little' People Who Changed U.S. History" Have students read the selection silently. Be sure students use the Check-ins to help them apply the strategy of using their prior knowledge. As they read, have them think about the title and why Brown, Gideon, and Miranda are called "little" people. Encourage students to mark the text, as active readers do. At the end of the selection, have students check any marks they have made. Decide if you want students to read aloud.

After You Read

B. Discuss students' prior knowledge of *Brown v. Board of Education.*

Extending the Reading Using an encyclopedia or other reference that contains the Constitution of the United States, help students read and interpret the 5th Amendment and Section 1 of the 14th Amendment, the legal bases for these three Supreme Court decisions.

Think About It: Apply Information Read the introductory paragraph.
A. Work through the guided practice orally with students.
B. Have students complete the Practice on their own.

Talk About It To help students track and organize their thoughts as they discuss, have them make a chart with column headings *Decision* and *Why* and row headings *Affects most people, Affects fewest people, Affects me most,* and *Affects me least.*

Extending the Skill Ask students what other rights they know U.S. citizens have. Compile a class list. Review the Bill of Rights, and have students decide which rights in the list are assured by each amendment. Ask students to think of situations in which they exercise these rights.

More Practice *Voyager 4 Workbook* p. 34

Write About It: Write Your Opinion Read the introduction and the three sample questions. Have students choose their own topic. List other suggested topics on the board if necessary.
A. Explain how to use the Idea Frame to help organize ideas. Students should know they can and should list more than two reasons if they wish. Tell them, however, that they should be able to support each reason with a fact or example from personal experience. You can also provide copies of PCM 7 for students to use.
B. Before they write their paragraphs, students can number the reasons in their Idea Frame to show the order in which they will write them. Have students date their writing and put it in their working folders.

Life Skill: Read a Bar Graph Read the introductory paragraph. Remind students of the single vertical bar graph in Lesson 7, page 81. Discuss similarities and differences between the two bar graphs.

Show students how to read the double bar graph. As you read the second paragraph aloud, have students point to the bars, the key, the years along the vertical axis, and the numbers along the horizontal axis in the graph. As you read the third paragraph, have them move their fingers along the bars and down. Ask which numbers they read. Read the fourth paragraph to see if students read the graph correctly.

Practice Have students complete this activity on their own. Discuss their responses.

Progress Evaluation Have students fill in copies of PCM 9 to include in their working folders.

Lesson 11 (p. 120)

Learning Goals Discuss the learning goals.

Before You Read Read and discuss the first two paragraphs. Ask students whether they ever like to read political cartoons or letters to the editor in the newspaper. Show them the cartoons and letters in a local newspaper. Point out that students will apply the strategy of setting a purpose as they read the political cartoon and letters to the editor.

Read the third paragraph and pre-reading activity. Encourage students to set a purpose for reading by choosing or writing a question they would like answered.

Preview the Reading Have students read the directions and preview the selection. Poll students for their predictions about which letters will agree or disagree with the cartoon. Tally the results on the board.

"Americans Held Hostage" Have students read the cartoon. Then discuss their answers to the questions.

"Letters to the Editor" Have students read the letters silently, marking the text, as active readers do. When they finish, have them check any marks they made. Have volunteers read the letters aloud. As students read each letter, have them determine whether it matches their prediction of agreeing or disagreeing with the cartoon. Tally the results on the board.

After You Read
B. Have students form pairs to discuss the questions.

Extending the Reading Have students group the letters to the editor into those that agree with the cartoon and those that do not. Ask them to list the various reasons given for or against the cartoon.

Think About It: Identify the Main Idea Read and discuss the first paragraph. Review the definition of the main idea as the most important point in a piece of writing. Discuss how students can read between the lines to determine an unstated main idea. Demonstrate with Yolanda Green's letter on page 122 of the student book. Show how each detail supports this main idea: Unlike the neighborhood described in the cartoon, the writer's neighborhood is safe because the people work to make it safe.
A. Read the first letter aloud. Ask students to underline the main idea and explain why it is the main idea before they read the answer. Read the second letter aloud. Ask volunteers to state the main idea and explain how they determined it. If necessary, model identifying the unstated main idea.
B. Ask students to complete the Practice on their own or with a partner.

Talk About It After students' discussion, compile a class list of their reasons for and reasons against each statement. If necessary, discuss the need for tolerance and respect for other people's opinions.

Extending the Skill Use PCM 2. Bring in news articles and letters to the editor from your local newspaper. Have students work in pairs to identify the main idea of the pieces they chose. Have students date their organizers and put them in their working folders.

More Practice *Voyager 4 Workbook* p. 36

Write About It: Write a Letter to the Editor Read the first paragraph. Have the class brainstorm to create a list of possible topics. Suggest that they think about problems in their neighborhood or community, their state, or the nation. Write the topics on the board, and have each student select one.
A. Provide copies of PCM 7 if students need more space for prewriting.
B. Go over the list of tips before students write their letters. Have students date their letters and put them in their working folders.

Life Skill: Analyze a Political Cartoon Read the introductory paragraphs aloud. Point out how much information students can learn by looking at the symbols, title, captions, and labels in political cartoons. Demonstrate with the cartoon "Americans Held Hostage." Then discuss "Barely Moving." See if students understand that the black-robed figure represents the U.S. justice system.

Practice Discuss students' answers to the questions to make sure students understand how to analyze a cartoon.

Talk About It Remind students to study the symbols, the title, the captions, and the labels to help them understand the cartoons they bring in. They might also want to display the cartoons after analyzing and discussing them.

Progress Evaluation Have students fill in copies of PCM 9 to include in their working folders.

Lesson 12 (p. 128)

Learning Goals Discuss the learning goals.

Before You Read Point out that students will practice the strategy of visualizing as they read the story in this lesson. Read the introductory paragraph and pre-reading activity. Have students describe what they see in their minds when they visualize a small convenience store. Then have students give reasons such a store would be easy to rob. List responses on the board.

Preview the Reading Have students read the directions and preview the selection. Record volunteers' predictions on the board.

"Crimebusters" Have students read the selection silently, using the Check-ins to help them apply the strategy of visualizing. Encourage students to mark the text, as active readers do. At the end of the selection, have students check any marks they have made. Note the shifts in tense between past and present. Explain to students that the story is being told in an informal manner, as if it were being spoken rather than written. Have volunteers read the story aloud.

Talk About It Discuss the meaning of the cartoon and students' answers to the questions in Talk About It. Tell students to support their opinions with facts and personal experiences. You may want to have students who believe one side of the issue explain their reasons, then have students on the other side do the same.

After You Read

B. Encourage students to share with a partner what they visualized about the story.

Extending the Reading Bring in a story about a robbery from your local newspaper. Ask students to visualize the events as you read. Then have students retell the main events in the story.

Think About It: Follow a Sequence of Events Read and discuss the first two paragraphs. Ask if students can suggest other time-related words that may act as clues to sequence. List these on the board.

A. Ask a volunteer to read the paragraph aloud. Compare the events in the story with the list of sequence of events.

B. Have students complete the Practice on their own. Discuss their sequences.

Talk About It Suggest that students list the main events in sequence and use their list to retell the story.

Extending the Skill Have students list in sequence the events in each of the three true stories in Lesson 10. Have them date their lists and put them in their working folders.

More Practice *Voyager 4 Workbook* p. 37

Write About It: Write a Poem Read and discuss the introduction. Ask students to visualize what the poet is describing about prison life as you read "The Artist." When you have finished reading, ask students what images they visualized and how the poem made them feel. You might also ask, *"When was the only time this inmate was allowed to be an artist? Why do you think this is so?"*

Read and discuss the two paragraphs on free verse and poetic techniques. Have students reread "The Artist." Note the poet's use of lowercase letters and short lines. Ask students what they think these devices tell them about the speaker in the poem. (The speaker may feel small and unimportant; he may lead a spare, bleak life; he may have a low opinion of himself.)

A. Ask students to think of a topic they would like to write about in a free-verse poem. If necessary, write a few topics on the board, and ask students to suggest others. When students have selected a topic, suggest they brainstorm or do free writing to get ideas for their poem. Then invite them to visualize images that would make their poems come alive. Encourage them to list as many words to describe these images as they can. They can go back and cross out or add ideas, images, and words as they like.

B. Have students draft their poems. They may use the poem starters suggested for "In My Dreams" or write the entire poem on their own. Ask volunteers to read their poems aloud. Have students date their poems and put them in their working folders.

Life Skill: Read a Parking Ticket Read and discuss the introductory paragraph. Ask students to examine the sample parking ticket and explain what information is given in each section. Have students answer the two questions aloud.

Practice Ask students to complete the Practice on their own.

Progress Evaluation Have students fill in copies of PCM 9 to include in their working folders.

Writing Skills Mini-Lesson: Using Apostrophes Correctly (p. 138)

1. Read the first rule and the two examples. Ask students to suggest other contractions, and list them on the board.
2. Read the second set of rules and their examples. Ask students to suggest other examples for each rule, and list them on the board. Be sure students read the tip and understand not to add an apostrophe to form a possessive pronoun or a plural noun. Using *'s* to form a plural is a very common mistake.

Practice Have students do the Practice on separate paper. They can fill in apostrophes before they recopy if they wish. Have students date their writing and put it in their working folders.

More Practice *Voyager 4 Workbook* pp. 39 and 43

Unit 4 Review (p. 139)

Follow the process described in Unit 1. When students get to the editing stage of the writing process, remind them to find and fix any fragments, run-on sentences, usage problems, and apostrophe problems.

More Practice *Voyager 4 Workbook* p. 40

Extending the Theme To extend the theme "Crime and the Law," provide or have students bring in cartoons about this topic. Give students copies of the cartoons without the captions. Have students write their own captions that sum up the cartoon's intent and also identify any symbols that are used. If a cartoon has more than one frame, have students create a sequence of events for the cartoon. Then have students match what they wrote with the original captions for the cartoons.

Final Note Review with students the copies of PCM 9 that they have completed for this unit. Ask what additional help they think they need with material from the three lessons and the Writing Skills Mini-Lesson in Unit 4. Discuss possible ways of meeting those needs.

Post-Assessment (p. 139)

When students have completed Unit 4, be sure they complete the Skills Review as well as Student Self-Assessment #2 found at the end of *Voyager 4*. (See Using the Skills Review on page 16 and Using the Student Self-Assessments on page 15.) Encourage them to evaluate their own reading and writing progress by comparing their answers with those they gave before beginning *Voyager 4*.

Alternative Assessment Follow the directions on PCM 10: Tips for Preparing a Progress Portfolio to help students evaluate the material in their working folders and assemble their progress portfolios. Then use PCM 11: Portfolio Conference Questionnaire as you conduct one-on-one evaluation conferences with students.

Voyager 5 Teacher's Notes

Pre-Assessment

Before you begin Unit 1 with students, have them complete the Student Self-Assessment and the Skills Preview at the beginning of *Voyager 5* (see Using the Student Self-Assessments, page 15, and Using the Skills Preview, page 15).

In addition to *Voyager 5,* students will need
• folders in which to keep their finished work and their work in progress (see Working Folders on page 7)
• a spiral-bound or three-ring notebook to use as a personal dictionary (see Personal Dictionaries on page 18)
• a spiral-bound or three-ring notebook to use as a personal spelling list (see page 20)

▶ Unit 1: Money Matters

Part of Unit	Voyager 5 pages	TRG pages	Workbook pages
Overview	13	42 – 43	
Lesson 1	14 – 23	43 – 44	4 – 5
Lesson 2	24 – 31	44 – 45	6
Lesson 3	32 – 41	45 – 47	7 – 8
Writing Skills Mini-Lesson	42	47	9
Unit 1 Review	43 – 44	47	10 – 13

Student Objectives

Reading
• Read two articles, a chart, and a bank signature card.
• Apply the reading strategies of setting a purpose, skimming, and using prior experience.
• Identify the main idea and details, understand categories, and recognize problems and solutions.

Writing
• Write an action plan, fill in a bank signature card, and write a short article.

Speaking and Listening
• Summarize, role-play, and interview.

Life Skill
• Read a circle graph, read a bank statement, and understand a budget.

▶ Unit 1 PCMs
PCM 1: KWHL Chart
PCM 2: Main Idea and Details Organizer
PCM 4: Problem/Solution Work Sheet
PCM 8: Strategies for Recognizing Words
PCM 9: Student Progress Tracking Sheet

▶ Personal Dictionaries and Spelling Lists
Encourage students to add words they would like to learn to their dictionaries and spelling lists during each lesson in Unit 1.

▶ Word Recognition Strategies If students need practice with recognizing words, distribute copies of PCM 8 for them to work with.

Unit 1 Overview (p. 13)

This overview introduces the theme "Money Matters" and encourages students to relate to it personally before they begin Lesson 1. Discuss how the art relates to the theme. Read the overview to students, or ask volunteers to read it aloud. Discuss students' answers to the questions.

Be an Active Reader Explain that experienced readers are "active" readers—they think about the information they are reading, and they try to figure out words and ideas they don't understand.

Encourage students to mark things they don't understand with question marks and to underline any words they don't know. Tell them they will return to any marks they make after they have finished reading the entire selection.

Lesson 1 (p. 14)

Learning Goals Discuss the learning goals. Explain that Lesson 1 will focus on these goals.

Before You Read Point out that students will apply the strategy of setting a purpose before they read the article in this lesson. Explain that experienced readers decide what they want to get out of a reading selection before they begin to read. Then they read to fulfill that purpose.

Read the paragraph aloud. Have students list two or three expenses they would like to reduce.

Have students use PCM 1 to identify what they already know about reducing expenses and what they would like to learn. Tell them to read to find ways to reduce the expenses they listed.

Preview the Reading Read the text, and demonstrate how to preview a reading. Then discuss the questions with students. Discuss the "house of cards" metaphor. Ask students if they have ever tried to build a house of cards.

Use the Strategy In Before You Read, students began working with a reading strategy. Use the Strategy encourages students to apply this strategy as they read. The Check-ins within the reading selection also remind students to apply the strategy as they read.

Read and discuss the text. Tell students to try to follow the directions as they read the article.

"What's Eating Your Paycheck?" Have students read the article silently. Explain how to use the footnotes to learn the definitions of selected words. Be sure students use the Check-ins to help them apply the strategy of setting a purpose. Encourage students to mark the text as explained in Be an Active Reader on page 13 of *Voyager 5*. Decide if and when you want students to read aloud. At the

end of the selection, have them reread sections they marked to see if they understand those sections now. If not, discuss the section with the student.

If students are unable to figure out the words they underlined, have them use PCM 8. If students are still unable to figure out the words, encourage them to use a dictionary.

Determine if students know how to use a dictionary. If not, demonstrate how and give students practice in looking up words, using the pronunciation guide, and determining which definition applies in the context of the reading.

"How Much Does a Car or Truck Cost?" This feature extends the ideas from "What's Eating Your Paycheck?" and teaches the practical skill of reading a circle graph. Read the text with students, and have them answer the questions posed in the text. Be sure they understand that the entire circle represents 100 percent of car or truck expenses, and that each section of the circle is a fraction of that 100 percent.

After You Read
A. Have students do this exercise independently and use the Answer Key to check their answers. Discuss any wrong answers. To improve students' reading comprehension skills, have them find evidence for the correct answers in the article.
B. Have students look at their answers in Before You Read to get them started. Ask them to list at least three ideas. Take some time to let students share and discuss their ideas with others.
C. Have students discuss the questions in pairs or small groups. Encourage them to consider their own experience and the experiences of family and friends as they answer the questions. Have students share their answers with the entire class. Encourage them to write their responses in a personal or dialogue journal. (See Working with Adult Student Writers, page 19.)

Have students fill in the last column of PCM 1 now.

Extending the Reading Discuss the costs of using credit cards: annual fees and finance charges on the unpaid portion of the balance. Discuss the dangers of using several cards and making only the minimum payment each month.

Think About It: Identify the Main Idea and Details
Read and discuss the introductory paragraphs. Using a copy of PCM 2, illustrate how the details of a paragraph support and relate to the main idea of the paragraph. Explain that in a longer piece of writing, the main ideas of all the paragraphs or sections are the details that support the main idea of the whole selection.

A. Read this section aloud as students follow along silently. Point out that each of the four details (the four remaining sentences) supports the main idea by suggesting a way to pay bills.

B. Have students do the Practice independently. Check their answers.

Extending the Skill
Use PCM 2. Ask students to write the main idea of "What's Eating Your Paycheck?" (the second sentence in the article), then to find five supporting details (the main ideas of the five sections of the article). Discuss the completed organizers with the group. Have students date their organizers and put them in their working folders.

Talk About It
Before students summarize the article for friends or family, have them practice by summarizing the article as a class. Suggest that they use the information they wrote on PCM 2 during the extension activity as notes.

More Practice
Voyager 5 Workbook p. 4. The workbook exercises are designed to be done independently. They should not require teacher input.

Write About It: Write an Action Plan
Read the first paragraph aloud.

A. Have students read the paragraph and the example. Ask them to target a spending area and to brainstorm ways to reduce spending in that area. Explain that when we brainstorm, we think quickly and creatively and write down all our ideas without judging them. When we are finished brainstorming, we go back and select the best ideas. Encourage students to brainstorm as many ways as they can to reduce

spending, then go back and select the three or four best ways.

B. Help students write a topic sentence. Tell them to use ideas they brainstormed during prewriting as supporting details in their paragraph. Encourage them to expand on the details by explaining not only what they will do but also when and how they will do it. Have students date their paragraphs and put them in their working folders.

Life Skill: A Closer Look at Reading a Circle Graph
Read the first paragraph. Ask, *"What is the title of this circle graph?"* (How Americans Spent Their Money in 1992) *"How many spending areas are shown?"* (7) *"If you add up all the percentages shown, what is the total?"* (100 percent) *"In which category do we spend the most money?"* (housing) Then have the class answer the question.

Practice
Have students do the Practice independently or in pairs. Check their answers.

Progress Evaluation
Have students fill in copies of PCM 9 to include in their working folders.

Lesson 2 (p. 24)

Learning Goals
Discuss the learning goals. Explain that Lesson 2 will focus on these goals.

Before You Read
Tell students that recalling what you already know about a subject can help you anticipate and better understand what you read about that subject. Read the paragraph, and ask students to list several words or terms about checking accounts or banking. List their responses on the board.

Preview the Reading
Read the text aloud, and demonstrate how to skim a reading. Then discuss the questions with students.

Use the Strategy
See Lesson 1 notes.

"Opening a Checking Account"
Have volunteers read the first two paragraphs. After paragraph 2, study the chart called "Types of Checking Accounts." Show students how to read a chart, reading down columns and across rows. Ask such

questions as, *"What is the monthly service charge for a personal checking account?"* ($8.00) to be sure they understand how to read the chart. Have students look at the bank signature card after paragraph 4. Encourage students to mark the text, as active readers do. At the end of the selection, have them check any marks they have made.

After You Read
A. See Lesson 1 notes.
B. Remind students that skimming means taking a brief look for something specific.
C. See Lesson 1 notes.

Extending the Reading Ask students to compile information on checking accounts from local banks. Divide the class into small groups, and assign each group a bank. Each group should find out what types of accounts its bank offers and what features define each account. Students can call for information or pick up brochures. Have each group create a chart like the one on page 25 of *Voyager 5* with enough rows and columns to accommodate all the different checking accounts its bank offers. Compile the charts in a kit or a notebook.

Think About It: Understand Categories Ask students to read the introductory paragraphs. Explain that they often sort things into categories (e.g., sorting laundry into white, light, and dark colors). Ask if students can think of other examples of everyday classifying (categories in a shopping list: groceries, household needs, drugstore items, etc.).
A. Read this section aloud as students follow along silently. Remind students to read down columns and across rows. Have students answer the question.
B. Have students do the Practice independently. Check their answers.

Talk About It Explain that role-playing like this helps build students' communication skills, which are vital to finding and keeping a job. Have them prepare for role-playing—the customer by listing questions; the bank employee by studying the information about the specific kind of account.

Extending the Skill Explain that categorizing information is an important part of managing money.

Ask students to think of personal spending categories (e.g., food, housing, utilities, transportation). Then have them group their own expenses under the appropriate categories (e.g., gas, electricity, and water under utilities; car payments, insurance premiums, and fuel under transportation). Students should list the names of their expenses but not the amounts. Have students date their lists and put them in their working folders. They may work further with these lists in a Lesson 3 extension activity.

More Practice *Voyager 5 Workbook* p. 6

Write About It: Fill In a Bank Signature Card Read the first paragraph aloud.
A. Students can make up the information requested if they prefer. Students who do not have a Social Security number can list any other identification number.
B. Have students fill in the form as directed. Be sure they print everything but the signature.

Life Skill: Read a Bank Statement Read the first paragraph. Explain that the Account Summary gives the current status of the account, while the Transactions are the checks, withdrawals, and deposits posted to the account during the month. To make sure students read the statement correctly, ask questions about it, such as *"On what date was check number 1054 posted?"* (6-8).

Practice Have students do the Practice independently or in pairs.

Progress Evaluation Have students fill in copies of PCM 9 to include in their working folders.

Lesson 3 (p. 32)

Learning Goals Discuss the learning goals. Explain that Lesson 3 will focus on these goals.

Before You Read Point out that students will practice the strategy of using their prior experience as they read the article. Explain that experienced readers draw on what they have seen, heard, and done to help them relate to and better understand their reading. In Lesson 3, students will read about the dreams and successes of different people around the world. By calling to mind their own dreams, students can compare their experiences with those they read about. Interacting with the text in this way increases reading comprehension.

Have students read the paragraph and discuss the questions in pairs or small groups.

Preview the Reading Have students read the directions and preview the selection. Provide a current world map or globe, and help students locate the places listed. Ask students to share anything they know about these places.

Use the Strategy See Lesson 1 notes.

"$100 Dreams" Have students read the article silently. Be sure they use the Check-ins to help them apply the strategy of using prior experience. Explain colloquial expressions (e.g., *hand-to-mouth*) if necessary. Ask students why *TUP* is an abbreviation for *Trickle Up Program*. Encourage students to mark the text, as active readers do. At the end of the selection, have them check any marks they have made. Decide if and when you want students to read aloud.

After You Read

A. See Lesson 1 notes.
B. Tell students to think of their own experiences as they evaluate each statement, then check whether they agree, disagree, or are not sure. Have them compare and discuss their answers.
C. See Lesson 1 notes.

Extending the Reading Ask students what help is offered to small-business owners in the United States. Elicit anything they already know about the Small Business Administration. Your local librarian should be able to help you obtain information. If students are interested, invite a spokesperson from the SBA to speak to the class.

Think About It: Recognize Problems and Solutions Read the first paragraph. Mention that self-help articles on topics such as "how to lose weight" and "how to discipline a child" are usually written in a problem/solution format: the problem is stated, then solutions are offered.

A. Ask students to read the first excerpt in question 1 and then try to identify the solution in the second excerpt before reading the answer. Then have them try to find the problem and solution in the excerpt in question 2. Discuss any problems students may have.
B. Explain that the ellipsis (. . .) at the beginning of excerpt 1 indicates that it doesn't include some words from the original version. Have students do the Practice independently. Check their answers.

Talk About It Poll students on the kinds of businesses they might be interested in. Encourage them to be realistic. Have students with similar business interests pair up or form small groups. As students discuss the questions, ask them to list start-up expenses as well as skills needed to run the business. Share responses with the group.

Extending the Skill Use PCM 4. Refer students to the reading selection in Lesson 1, "What's Eating Your Paycheck?" Ask pairs of students to analyze the article from a problem/solution viewpoint, identifying money problems, the causes of those problems, and possible solutions to them. Have students date their work sheets and put them in their working folders.

More Practice *Voyager 5 Workbook* p. 7

Write About It: Write a Short Article Read the first paragraph aloud.

A. If possible, line up several business people who would be willing to be interviewed in person or by telephone. Help students list the questions they will ask. Remind students to take careful notes as they conduct the interview.
B. Have students follow the directions as they write their articles. Explain that their second paragraph need not answer all of the questions posed; the questions are just suggested topic areas. Have students date their articles and put them in their working folders.

Life Skill: Understand a Budget Read the first paragraph with students, and discuss the sample budget. Explain that the budgeted amount is *predicted* spending, and the money spent is the *actual* spending. Ask students how they would answer the question in the text.

Practice Have students do the Practice independently. Discuss their responses.

Extending the Life Skill Encourage students to create their own monthly budgets. Have them list their fixed expenses such as mortgage or rent, as well as estimated expenses such as groceries and gas. Ask students to track their expenses for the upcoming month and compare their budgeted amount with the actual amount spent. Assure students that their budgets are private and that they need not share them.

Progress Evaluation Have students fill in copies of PCM 9 to include in their working folders.

Writing Skills Mini-Lesson: Capitalization Rules (p. 42)

Explain that correct capitalization helps other people read and understand one's writing more easily.
1. Read this rule with students.
2–5. Read these rules one at a time, and ask students to name other examples for each. Write their examples on the board.

Practice Have students complete the Practice on their own. Check their completed paragraphs as a class, matching each capital letter with a rule. Have students date their work and put it in their working folders.

More Practice *Voyager 5 Workbook* pp. 9 and 13

Unit 1 Review (p. 43)

Explain that this review will help students evaluate what they have learned in Unit 1.

Reading Review Have students do the Reading Review independently. Have them check their answers against the Answer Key.

Writing Process Before students begin the Writing Review, have them turn to page 160 in *Voyager 5*. Discuss the writing process. Explain that students

have already completed stages 1 and 2 for each piece of writing they have done in Unit 1. Ask students to choose the draft they would like to work with further.

To give students specific direction in revising, go over the questions at the bottom of page 44 in the student book. To give students direction in editing, have them refer to the Writing Skills pages in the Reference Handbook (pages 156–159 in *Voyager 5*). Work with students as they revise, edit, and create a final draft. When they get to the editing stage, remind students to find and fix any errors in capitalization. Have students date their writing and put it in their working folders.

More Practice *Voyager 5 Workbook* p. 10

Extending the Theme To extend the theme "Money Matters," explore with the class the topic of saving money. Have students research various savings options offered by local banks, as they did with checking accounts in the Lesson 2 extension activity. Compile their charts in a notebook for the class to use as a reference. Discuss the reasons for saving (emergency, large or special purchases, college for children, retirement) and the importance of saving.

Final Note Review with students the copies of PCM 9 that they have completed for this unit. Ask what additional help they think they need with the material from the three lessons and the Writing Skills Mini-Lesson in Unit 1. Discuss possible ways of meeting those needs.

▶ Unit 2: On the Job

Part of Unit	Voyager 5 pages	TRG pages	Workbook pages
Overview	45	48	
Lesson 4	46 – 55	48 – 49	14 – 15
Lesson 5	56 – 63	49 – 50	16
Lesson 6	64 – 73	51	17 – 18
Writing Skills Mini-Lesson	74	51 – 52	19
Unit 2 Review	75 – 76	52	20 – 23

Student Objectives

Reading

- Read personal accounts, a poem, a work order and diagram, and memos.
- Apply the reading strategies of imagining, using prior experience, and using prior knowledge.
- Make inferences, follow steps in a process, and identify facts and opinions.

Writing

- Write a personal account, directions, and a memo.

Speaking and Listening

- Read aloud, give and receive directions, and summarize.

Life Skill

- Read workplace signs and symbols, a diagram, a time sheet, and an invoice.

▶ Unit 2 PCMs

PCM 4: Problem/Solution Work Sheet
PCM 8: Strategies for Recognizing Words
PCM 9: Student Progress Tracking Sheet

▶ Personal Dictionaries and Spelling Lists

Encourage students to add words they would like to learn to their dictionaries and spelling lists during each lesson in Unit 2.

▶ Word Recognition Strategies

If students need practice with recognizing words, distribute copies of PCM 8 for them to work with.

See Lesson 1 notes for lesson segments not addressed in these notes.

Unit 2 Overview (p. 45)

This overview introduces the theme "On the Job" and encourages students to relate to it personally before they begin the unit. Call attention to the art, and discuss how it relates to the theme. Read the overview to students, or ask volunteers to read it aloud. Discuss students' answers to the questions.

Be an Active Reader See Unit 1 notes.

Lesson 4 (p. 46)

Learning Goals Discuss the learning goals.

Before You Read Read the first two paragraphs. Point out that students will use the strategy of imagining to better understand the readings in this lesson. Explain that when they read, experienced readers imagine how the characters look and feel as events unfold. Have students answer the three questions.

Preview the Reading Have students read the directions and preview the selection. Record their predictions.

"I'm Not Making Coffee" and "Myrtle" Have students read the selections silently. Remind students that poets choose their words carefully for the way they sound and for the pictures they evoke. Be sure students use the Check-ins to help them apply the strategy of imagining. Encourage them to mark the text, as active readers do. At the end of the selections, have them check any marks they have made. Then have volunteers read the selections aloud.

After You Read

A. If students need help with question 5, ask, *"What does Myrtle do with the newspapers* (wraps them in plastic) *and how does she do it?"* (neatly)

B. Have students review their answers in Before You Read. Ask them to use their imagination as they complete the checklist. Note that there are no right or wrong answers for this exercise, but ask students to give reasons to support their answers.

Extending the Reading Analyze "Myrtle" with the class. Ask, *"What picture of Myrtle do you see in your mind? Why does the poet compare Myrtle to a candle flame?"* (She is dressed in bright yellow; he sees her as flickering through the rain.) Ask students to write a brief description of a worker they know, comparing this worker to an everyday object, as the poet compared Myrtle to a candle flame. Have volunteers share their completed descriptions. Have them date their descriptions and put them in their working folders.

Think About It: Make Inferences Read the introductory paragraphs with students. Discuss the clues in the first excerpt that imply that Bob is a cabdriver.

A. 1. Read the numbered paragraph and excerpt, and ask students what answer they inferred to the question. Discuss the answer given in the student book.

    2. Follow the process above. Then read the question that follows the given answer and discuss students' responses. Emphasize the final sentence. Often more than one appropriate inference can be made.

B. Have students do the Practice independently. Check their answers.

Talk About It As they discuss the questions, ask students to note what kind of job each person has and his or her responses. Have students share and compare what they have found with the class.

Extending the Skill Reread the selection "Making a Difference" in the Skills Preview. Demonstrate how an experienced reader makes inferences. Read the first paragraph, and note the inferences you can make: (1) The author calls the prisoners "strong"

people "just trying to make it." You can infer she is sympathetic to them. (2) When the book gives her an idea, you can infer she is a resourceful person. (3) She gets excited about a way to improve the prisoners' situation. You can infer she cares about her work. As you continue reading the selection, ask students what inferences can be made. Discuss inferences that can be made about the author's health.

More Practice *Voyager 5 Workbook* p. 14

Write About It: Write a Personal Account Read the first paragraph aloud.

A. Have volunteers read "What I Do at Work." Note that the personal account gives details about what the author does and when he does it.

    Have students choose a topic, such as "The Work I Do at Home." Encourage them to list all of their tasks in sequence if possible.

B. Remind students to follow the directions to produce drafts. Have them date their accounts and put them in their working folders.

Life Skill: Read Workplace Signs and Symbols

Read and discuss the first paragraph.

A. Have students read each of the signs and discuss where they might see them.

B–C. Discuss where the words and symbol might be seen.

Ask students to copy any signs or symbols they have seen but don't understand. Try to identify them for students.

Practice Have students work in pairs. Ask them to tell where they might see each of these signs.

Progress Evaluation Have students fill in copies of PCM 9 to include in their working folders.

Lesson 5 (p. 56)

Learning Goals Discuss the learning goals.

Before You Read Point out that students will use their prior experience with making repairs to better understand the reading. Read the first two paragraphs. Explain that students' repairs can be simple (e.g., replacing a light bulb or a battery) or more complex (e.g., replacing a flat tire or fixing an appliance). Have them think of this repair as they do the checklist.

Preview the Reading Have students read the directions and preview the selection.

"First Day on the Job: The Self-Taught Plumber"
Have students read the selection silently. Be sure they use the Check-ins to help them use their prior experience. If needed, explain that the work order is a written request for maintenance. Go over each step of the diagram sequentially with students. Encourage students to mark the text, as active readers do. Have them check any marks they have made when they finish reading.

After You Read
B. Name the strategy that works best for you. Discuss the strategy most helpful to each student. Point out that different strategies work best for different people, and people should use what works best for them.

C. Encourage students to evaluate the strategies and discover which strategy works best for them. Tell them to use that strategy most often.

Extending the Reading Discuss types of practical and job-related information found in a library. For instance, library resources can help a person
• find a job (newspaper want ads, career information, information on specific companies)
• build job skills (books on computers; books to help build reading, writing, math, and communication skills)
• make repairs and build things (how-to manuals and books)

If possible, visit your public library with students. Help students use the card or computer catalog to find career resources and how-to books. Encourage students to apply for a library card if they have not already done so.

Think About It: Follow Steps in a Process Read the first section aloud. After you have read "How to Send a Fax," ask students to close their books and tell the four steps in order.

A. Read as students follow along silently. Have students answer the question before reading the answer in the text.

B. Have students do the Practice independently. Check their answers.

Talk About It Encourage students to think of ways that help them understand oral directions (e.g., listening for signal words such as *first* and *last;* writing the steps down; doing each step as you hear it). Compile a class list of listening strategies.

Extending the Skill Bring in several sets of text-based directions (e.g., manuals on how to use a microwave or an answering machine; directions on how to print a computer file).

Have students work in pairs. Give each pair a set of directions. Ask students to read the directions and then write the steps in scrambled order. Have them exchange the scrambled directions with another pair and number each other's scrambled directions in correct order. Have them check their work against the original set of directions.

More Practice *Voyager 5 Workbook* p. 16

Write About It: Write Directions Read the first paragraph aloud. Explain that a flowchart is a special diagram that shows the "flow," or direction, of steps in a process.
A. Be sure students recognize the correct order of steps in the flowchart. Have students construct their flowcharts independently.
B. Let students write independently. Be sure they check their lists for accuracy. Have students date their directions and put them in their working folders.

Life Skill: Read a Diagram Read the first paragraph. Point out the parts list and how the coded parts appear in the illustration. To be sure students can read the diagram, ask questions such as, *"Which part is the glass?"* (part H) *"Where is it found in the diagram?"*

Practice Have students work in pairs as they study the diagram and complete the exercise.

Progress Evaluation Have students fill in copies of PCM 9 to include in their working folders.

Lesson 6 (p. 64)

Learning Goals Discuss the learning goals.

Before You Read Read the first three paragraphs with students. Have the class brainstorm possible memo topics, such as holidays, upcoming meetings, promotions, or changes in personnel. List them on the board. Read the fourth paragraph. Point out that students will use their prior knowledge about memos and business situations to help them understand the memos in this lesson.

Preview the Reading Have students read the directions and preview the selection. Discuss their answers to the questions.

"Problem Solving on the Job" Have students read the memos silently. Be sure students use the Check-ins to help them use their prior knowledge. Note the passage of time indicated by the dates on the memos. Encourage students to mark the text, as active readers do. Have them check any marks they have made when they finish reading.

After You Read
B. If needed, help students brainstorm ideas.

Extending the Reading Ask students to think of a safety problem they have encountered at work or at home. Have them use PCM 4 to identify and evaluate solutions to the problem. Have students date their work sheets and put them in their working folders.

Think About It: Identify Facts and Opinions Read the first section with students. Ask volunteers for other examples of facts and opinions.
A. 1. Read and discuss the questions, sample statements, and explanation.
    2. Read the questions and sample statements. Discuss students' choices for each statement.
B. Have students do the Practice independently. Discuss their answers.

Talk About It Help students evaluate each other's summaries constructively. Have them answer such questions as, "Are all the important details in the summary? If not, what else should be included? Are there any unimportant details?"

Extending the Skill Ask students to write three or more statements, including at least one fact and one opinion. Volunteers can read their statements, and the class can decide whether the statements are facts or opinions.

More Practice *Voyager 5 Workbook* p. 17

Write About It: Write a Memo Read the first paragraph.
A. Encourage students to think of work-related problems. Be sure they suggest several solutions for the problem. Have them brainstorm solutions on another sheet of paper if necessary, then go back and evaluate the solutions. Students may want to use the copies of PCM 4 they used for Extending the Reading.
B. Be sure students understand the structure of the memo they are to write. Have them date their memos and put them in their working folders.

Life Skill: Read a Time Sheet and an Invoice Students who are familiar with time sheets can study this one and do Practice A independently. Read the explanatory material and discuss it with students who have never used a time sheet.

Read the description of an invoice and discuss the form before students do Practice B.

Progress Evaluation Have students fill in copies of PCM 9 to include in their working folders.

Writing Skills Mini-Lesson: Making Subjects and Verbs Agree (p. 74)

To successfully complete this lesson, students must understand *subject, verb,* and *present tense.* Review these concepts. The rules on this page explain subject-verb agreement in the present tense. Stress the fact that the endings *-s* or *-es* are added only to third-person singular verbs in the present tense.
1. Read the rule. Explain that *he, she,* and *it* are singular pronouns. Read the examples. Point out the subjects in boldface type. Add other examples; ask students to name the subject and verb in each.

2. Read the rule and the examples. Add others, and have students name the subject and verb. Remind students that the endings -s or -es are added to verbs only when the subjects are singular nouns or third-person singular pronouns.

3. The verb *to be* is especially difficult because it has so many forms. Read the rule and the chart. Ask students to read the chart aloud as a group. Explain that for formal writing and speaking, it is important to use this verb correctly. Provide more practice exercises for students who use these forms incorrectly. Keep in mind that generally we write as we speak, and speech habits are particularly hard to change.

Practice Ask students to exchange their completed sentences with a partner. Have partners read the sentences aloud and correct them together. Then have students date their writing and put it in their working folders.

More Practice *Voyager 5 Workbook* pp. 19 and 23

Unit 2 Review (p. 75)

See Unit 1 notes. When students get to the editing stage in the writing process, remind them to find and fix errors in capitalization and subject-verb agreement.

More Practice *Voyager 5 Workbook* p. 20

Extending the Theme To extend the theme "On the Job," ask students to briefly discuss jobs they have had. How did they get the jobs? What tasks did they do? What were the hours and the working conditions? If students have not had paid jobs, ask them to describe their unpaid work or jobs that friends have held. Compile a class job guide; include in the guide students' job titles and descriptions.

Final Note Review with students the copies of PCM 9 that they have completed for this unit. Ask what additional help they think they need with material from the three lessons and the Writing Skills Mini-Lesson in Unit 2. Discuss possible ways of meeting those needs.

▶ Unit 3: Making a Difference

Part of Unit	Voyager 5 pages	TRG pages	Workbook pages
Overview	77	53	
Lesson 7	78 – 87	53 – 55	24 – 25
Lesson 8	88 – 95	55 – 56	26
Lesson 9	96 – 105	56 – 57	27 – 28
Writing Skills Mini-Lesson	106	57	29
Unit 3 Review	107 – 108	57	30 – 33

Student Objectives

Reading

- Read a biography, a short story, a voter registration form, letters to the editor, and bar graphs.
- Apply the reading strategies of predicting content, skimming, and using prior knowledge.
- Summarize information, categorize information, and identify facts and opinions.

Writing

- Write an autobiography, a persuasive letter, and a letter to the editor.

Speaking and Listening

- Tell a story, interview, and discuss.

Life Skill

- Read a brochure, community announcements, and bar graphs.

▶ Unit 3 PCMs

PCM 4: Problem/Solution Work Sheet
PCM 7: Idea Map
PCM 8: Strategies for Recognizing Words
PCM 9: Student Progress Tracking Sheet

▶ Personal Dictionaries and Spelling Lists

Encourage students to add words they would like to learn to their dictionaries and spelling lists during each lesson in Unit 3.

▶ Word Recognition Strategies

If students need practice with recognizing words, distribute copies of PCM 8 for them to work with.

See Lesson 1 notes for lesson segments not addressed in these notes.

Unit 3 Overview (p. 77)

The overview introduces the theme "Making a Difference" and encourages students to relate to it personally before they begin the unit. Call attention to the art, and discuss how it relates to the theme. Have volunteers read the overview. Discuss the questions.

Be an Active Reader See Unit 1 notes.

Lesson 7 (p. 78)

Learning Goals Discuss the learning goals.

Before You Read Have students read the first paragraph. Emphasize that a biography is an account of a person's life. Authors often write biographies of famous people. Ask students to name biographies they may have read or heard about.

Introduce the strategy of predicting content as students read the biography. Explain that based on what they know about the type of reading, readers can predict what might be in the selection. Then they look for that information as they read. They also think about what they have just read to predict what they are going to read next.

Read the second paragraph with students and ask, *"If you told someone's life story, what details would you include?"* Have them write two more predictions and share them with the group.

Preview the Reading Have students read the directions and preview the selection. As students preview, ask, *"How does the writer organize the information about Shirley Chisholm's life?"* (point out the subheads in the reading). Have students write their predictions and share the predictions with the group.

"Shirley Chisholm: First Black Congresswoman"

Have students read the selection silently. Be sure students use the Check-ins to help them apply the strategy of predicting content. Encourage students to mark the text, as active readers do. At the end of the selection, have them check any marks they have made.

After You Read

B. Have students review the predictions they made in Before You Read. Encourage them to list three new things without referring to the biography.

C. Suggest that students consider leaders and politicians they admire as they list qualities for the first question.

Extending the Reading Encourage students to read about other people who have made a difference in some way. Bring to class biographies or biographical articles suitable for readers at this level. (Such books can be found in the new-readers section of public libraries, at literacy resource centers, and through New Readers Press.) Have students pick a biography that interests them, and ask them to read it on their own time. Students can share what they learned in Extending the Skill (see this page).

Think About It: Summarize Information Read the introduction. Emphasize that a summary should be brief and in students' own words.

A. Have students read this section. Point out the differences in wording between the sample summary and the words in the original selection.

B. Have students do the Practice independently. Encourage them to include only the most important details. If necessary, help students write a topic sentence for each paragraph.

Remind students to make sure they listed events in the correct order. You may want to have students exchange summaries with a partner and evaluate each other's work. Have students date their summaries and put them in their working folders.

Talk About It Ask students to make notes and organize their thoughts before they share the life stories with a partner or with the whole group. If students are reading a biography (see Extending the Reading, this page), invite them to discuss the person they chose to read about. Have students answer the question, "What did this person do to make a difference?"

Extending the Skill Have students write brief summaries of the biographies they read in Extending the Reading (see this page). For those students who have not read biographies, provide an appropriate magazine or newspaper human interest article for them to summarize. Or have students summarize "$100 Dreams" in Lesson 3.

More Practice *Voyager 5 Workbook* p. 24

Write About It: Write an Autobiography Read the first paragraph aloud. Point out that *auto* means "self" in Greek. Give other examples of words with this prefix (e.g., *automobile*, "self-moving"; *autograph*, "self-written").

A. Have students read and follow the directions. Students can use different headings, such as *childhood* and *teen years*, or different places they have lived.

B. Encourage students to add details to their prewriting lists to make their paragraphs more interesting. Have students date their autobiographies and put them in their working folders.

Life Skill: Read a Brochure Read the explanatory paragraphs with students. Have students read the brochure silently or out loud. Point out such features as the bulleted list and the use of color type that are commonly used in brochures to highlight important information.

Practice Have students work independently. Check their answers.

Extending the Life Skill Ask students to work in pairs or small groups to create a one-page brochure advertising your school or program. Have them brainstorm the important facts they want to convey. Then have them write in a style similar to the one used in the brochure in the student book: short, direct text; bulleted list; catchy title. Encourage them to use their artistic skills in creating a layout for their text. Display the completed brochures in your classroom or elsewhere in the building.

Progress Evaluation Have students fill in copies of PCM 9 to include in their working folders.

Lesson 8 (p. 88)

Learning Goals Discuss the learning goals.

Before You Read Read the paragraph aloud. Tell students to list anything about voting that comes to mind, negative or positive. Have volunteers share their lists.

Preview the Reading Point out that students will apply the strategy of skimming before they read. Remind them that skimming is another way to preview. Have students read the directions and skim the selection. Discuss their answers to the questions.

"A New Voter in the West End" Have students read the selection silently. Be sure students use the Check-ins and read the definitions of difficult words. Encourage them to mark the text, as active readers do. At the end of the selection, have them check any marks they have made.

After You Read
B. Discuss how skimming can help readers understand reading material (readers have an idea of the content and know what to expect, so they can focus more on the details).

Extending the Reading Obtain voter registration forms for your state. Forms should be available at the public library, at city hall, or from the League of Women Voters. Go over the form with students. Explain how citizens can register if they are not already registered voters.

Think About It: Categorize Information Have students read the explanatory section. Ask, *"What are the three categories Rosa uses?"*
A. 1–2. Read each numbered paragraph. Have students study each form and decide how the information would be categorized.

B. Have students do the Practice independently or in pairs. Discuss their answers.

Talk About It Tell students that they should interview three people who are not class members. Remind students to record their interview results carefully. Have the class tally all the responses on one chart in columns headed *Yes* and *No*. Ask, *"Did most of the people you interviewed have the same opinion, or did the opinions vary?"*

Discuss the questions in small groups or as a class.

Extending the Skill Let students categorize simple, everyday information. On a board or flip chart, randomly list the names of several colors, cities, holidays, famous people, and movies or TV shows. Have at least two items in each category. Ask students to put the information into categories that they name. Have students compare their categories when they've finished. Explain that different categories are not right or wrong—just different.

More Practice *Voyager 5 Workbook* p. 26

Write About It: Write a Persuasive Letter Read the first paragraph aloud. Explain that *to persuade* means to get someone to agree with you, and that persuasion usually requires clear, valid arguments.
A. As students read the sample letter, point out how the writer stated the problem clearly and then offered two solutions. If students need help choosing topics, suggest common topics, such as traffic control, public transportation, crime, and city maintenance. If students need help thinking of solutions, have them brainstorm with partners.
B. Remind students to state the problem clearly and to support their solution with reasons why it would work. Have students date their letters and put them in their working folders.

Life Skill: Read Community Announcements Read the explanatory paragraph, and have students read the announcement. Discuss how the announcement features the basic facts about the speech as well as two attention-getting sentences (the first and next-to-last lines).

Practice Have students do the Practice independently; then go over the answers with the group.

Progress Evaluation Have students fill in copies of PCM 9 to include in their working folders.

Lesson 9 (p. 96)

Learning Goals Discuss the learning goals.

Before You Read Read the first paragraph. Point out that students will use their prior knowledge as they read the letters. Read the second paragraph, and have students name volunteer activities they remember from school. You may want them to brainstorm ways volunteers could have helped in their schools.

Preview the Reading Have students read the directions and preview the selection.

"Letters to the Editor: Volunteers in School" Have students read the letters silently. Decide if and when you want students to read aloud. Be sure students use the Check-ins to help them use their prior knowledge. Encourage students to mark the text, as active readers do, and go back to check any marks they have made.

"Why Volunteers Are Needed" Read the first paragraph and study the graphs as a class. Ask, *"What is the title of each graph? What do the numbers on the left represent? What does each bar represent?"*

After You Read
B. Encourage students to use their own or their children's experiences as they number their preferences.
C. Ask students to share tips they may have for helping children to learn and to feel good about learning. Gather the tips into a "tip sheet" or brochure.

Extending the Reading Have students work in groups to identify a problem related to education. Have them use PCM 4 to identify one or more causes of the problem and brainstorm possible solutions. Ask them to think specifically about what parents can do to help solve the problem. Have groups share their results.

Think About It: Identify Facts and Opinions Have students read the explanatory section.

A. 1–2. Read each numbered paragraph and the sample statements that follow. Ask students whether each statement is fact or opinion, and why. Discuss their responses.
B. Have students do the Practice independently. Discuss their answers.

Talk About It Students' opinions may vary. Some may feel that volunteers can help with academics, while others may think this is not appropriate. Mention other possible areas, such as field trips, gym or recess help, library work, and office support. Encourage students to support their opinions with facts. When discussion is finished, have note-takers compile lists of facts and opinions.

Extending the Skill Bring in letters to the editor from the newspaper. Have students work in pairs to read the letters and identify which statements in them are facts and which are opinions.

More Practice *Voyager 5 Workbook* p. 27

Write About It: Write a Letter to the Editor Read the first paragraph aloud.
A. Ask students to read the sample letter. Point out how the first paragraph clearly states the solution, while paragraphs 2 and 3 provide reasons. Have students identify the facts and opinions offered as reasons.

Help students choose a problem they want to write about. Remind them to think of reasons that support their proposed solution. Students might find PCM 7 helpful in organizing their ideas.

B. Make sure students understand what the body of their letter should be. Remind them to include a salutation, a closing, and their signature.

Life Skill: A Closer Look at a Bar Graph Read the first two paragraphs with students.
A. **Practice** Go over the graph with students to be sure they understand how to read it. Ask such questions as, *"What is the title? What do the numbers on the left represent? What do the bars represent?"* Have them do the exercise. Read and discuss the next paragraph.

B. Practice Explain how to use the key to read the double bar graph. Ask questions like the ones mentioned above. Have students complete the exercise and check their answers in the Answer Key.

Extending the Life Skill Bring a variety of bar graphs to class. Have students work in pairs. Give each pair two graphs to study and discuss. Ask students to name these features:
• the topic of the graph
• the items being shown or compared
• the items of greatest and least value on the graph

Pairs should exchange graphs to be sure they are reading both graphs correctly.

Progress Evaluation Have students fill in copies of PCM 9 to include in their working folders.

Writing Skills Mini-Lesson: More on Making Subjects and Verbs Agree (p. 106)

Review what students studied about subject-verb agreement in Unit 2. Read the first paragraph. Be sure students understand *subject, verb,* and *present tense.* Review the present tense forms of the verb *to be.*

1. Read the explanation and the examples. Explain that students must consider the compound subject as a whole, not just the word closest to the verb, when determining which verb form to use. Ask for examples of sentences with singular subjects; have the class turn them into compound subjects and change the verb accordingly.
2. Read the rule. Explain that interrupting words are often words that describe the subject. Write other examples on the board. Have students cross out the interrupting words and underline the subject and verb.

Practice Ask students to exchange their completed sentences with a partner. Have partners read the sentences aloud and correct them together. Have students date their writing and put it in their working folders.

More Practice *Voyager 5 Workbook* pp. 29 and 33

Unit 3 Review (p. 107)

See Unit 1 notes. When students get to the editing stage of the writing process, remind them to find and fix errors in capitalization and subject-verb agreement.

More Practice *Voyager 5 Workbook* p. 30

Extending the Theme To extend the theme "Making a Difference," invite each student to speak about a person who has made a difference, either in the student's own life or in people's lives in general (e.g., a politician, athlete, or other celebrity). Have students prepare their speeches. Remind students what they learned about summarizing: they should include the main point—how the person made a difference—as well as important details that support the main point.

Final Note Review with students the copies of PCM 9 that they have completed for this unit. Ask what additional help they think they need with material from the three lessons and the Writing Skills Mini-Lesson in Unit 3. Discuss possible ways of meeting those needs.

▶ Unit 4: Many Cultures

Part of Unit	Voyager 5 pages	TRG pages	Workbook pages
Overview	109	58	
Lesson 10	110 – 119	58 – 60	34 – 35
Lesson 11	120 – 127	60 – 61	36
Lesson 12	128 – 137	61 – 62	37 – 38
Writing Skills Mini-Lesson	138	62	39
Unit 4 Review	139 – 140	62 – 63	40 – 43

Student Objectives

Reading
- Read fables, a diary entry, and an essay.
- Apply the reading strategies of imagining, using prior experience, and setting a purpose.
- Compare and contrast, make inferences, and identify the main idea and details.

Writing
- Write a fable, a diary entry, and an essay.

Speaking and Listening
- Tell a story, discuss, and summarize.

Life Skill
- Read a map, a schedule, and a chart.

▶ Unit 4 PCMs
PCM 1: KWHL Chart
PCM 2: Main Idea and Details Organizer
PCM 6: Comparison/Contrast Grid
PCM 8: Strategies for Recognizing Words
PCM 9: Student Progress Tracking Sheet

▶ Personal Dictionaries and Spelling Lists
Encourage students to add words they would like to learn to their dictionaries and spelling lists during each lesson in Unit 4.

▶ Word Recognition Strategies
If students need practice with recognizing words, distribute copies of PCM 8 for them to work with.

See Lesson 1 notes for lesson segments not addressed in these notes.

Unit 4 Overview (p. 109)

The overview introduces the theme "Many Cultures" and encourages students to relate to it personally before they begin the unit. Call attention to the art, and discuss how it relates to the theme. Have volunteers read the overview. Discuss the questions.

Be an Active Reader See Unit 1 notes.

Lesson 10 (p. 110)

Learning Goals Discuss the learning goals.

Before You Read Have students read the first paragraph. Ask them to name any fables they know. If students can't think of any fables, briefly tell them the outline of a fable such as "The Grasshopper and the Ant": The grasshopper danced through the summer, while the ant worked hard to store up food for the winter. When winter came, the grasshopper was starving and pleaded with the ant for food. Explain that fables often end in a moral or lesson. Ask students what they think the moral of this fable might be ("Don't live just for today. Plan for the future.").

Discuss how animals in fables represent certain human characteristics that we attribute to them. For instance, we perceive eagles to be proud and noble, turtles slow and plodding, and foxes sly.

Read the second paragraph. Point out that students will use the strategy of imagining as they read the fables. Model this activity by choosing an animal, such as a lion, and answering the questions aloud. Then invite students to do the same.

Preview the Reading Have students read the directions and preview the selections. Discuss their answers to the questions. Students may be familiar with the story of the hare and the tortoise; encourage them to use what they know about this tale as they make predictions about the other fables.

"The Eagle and the Spider" and other fables Be sure students use the Check-ins to help them apply the strategy of imagining as they read silently. Encourage students to mark the text, as active readers do. Have volunteers read the fables aloud and discuss them. After the second and third fables, discuss how each story illustrates its moral.

After You Read

B. Encourage students to add other adjectives to describe how they might feel.

C. You may also ask students to consider this question: *"When trying to teach someone about life, what strategies do you use? Do you give them advice, or let them learn through experience, or both? Why?"*

Extending the Reading

1. Point out that these fables come from three different areas of the world: Russia, Greece, and North America. Ask, *"Why do you think people from around the world have such similar stories?"* Encourage students to express and discuss their opinions. Bring in other fables so students can read them and look for similarities.

2. Suggest that students with children read fables to them.

Think About It: Compare and Contrast Introduce this skill by comparing and contrasting two famous people, for instance: *"Let's compare Jodie Foster and Denzel Washington. How are they alike?"* (Both are actors; both make movies; both have won Academy Awards for acting.) *"Let's contrast them. How are they different?"* (Foster is female, Washington is male; Foster is white, Washington black.) On the board, make a chart like the one in the student book and list students' answers.

Have students read the explanatory paragraphs and chart. Emphasize that comparing means looking

for similarities; contrasting means looking for differences.

A. Read with students, and have them answer the question in the text.

B. Have students do the Practice independently. Check their answers.

Talk About It Have students think of a time when they learned a meaningful lesson, either as a child or as an adult. You may need to offer a story about yourself as an example. Suggest they list the key events so they can be sure they tell them in order.

Extending the Skill As students work in pairs to compare their stories in Talk About It, have them use PCM 6. Demonstrate how to use the PCM by using one pair's stories: make one partner's story Subject 1 and the other's Subject 2.

More Practice *Voyager 5 Workbook* p. 34

Write About It: Write a Fable Have students read the first paragraph.

A. Read this section and go over the chain of events with students. Have students work with partners. They can begin prewriting by choosing the lesson, or moral, they want to illustrate. Their lessons can be common proverbs, such as, "The early bird gets the worm," "A stitch in time saves nine," "While the cat's away, the mice will play," or "Waste not, want not."

After partners have chosen a lesson or moral, have them develop a story for it. Encourage them to use animals that can demonstrate the qualities needed to teach their lesson. In the example, the German shepherd can stand for a bully who is used to getting his way. The poodle can stand for a small person who knows when it is smart to beat a retreat.

When partners are completing the chain of events, tell them that it is just a bare outline of what happens in the fable. They will add dialogue and details when they write the fable.

B. Have partners write fables based on their chain of events. Have them model their fables on the four fables in the lesson. Remind students to follow the tips in the bulleted list. Be sure they end their fable with the lesson learned. Have students date their fables and put them in their working folders.

Life Skill: Read a Map Read the two paragraphs with students. If students are fairly familiar with maps, let them study the map and move straight to the Practice. However, if students are unfamiliar with maps, you will need a more detailed explanation and discussion. If you have a globe available, use that also. Have students locate the seven continents and the United States. Ask students to name the ocean on each side of North America, and be sure they can read the compass correctly.

Practice Be sure students have answered question 1 correctly before they go on. Have them check their answers in the Answer Key.

Progress Evaluation Have students fill in copies of PCM 9 to include in their working folders.

Lesson 11 (p. 120)

Learning Goals Discuss the learning goals.

Before You Read Read the first paragraph. Ask students to explain the phrase "former Soviet Union." If they need help, explain that it was a nation that included 15 republics in Eastern Europe and northern Asia. It had a Communist government. Russia was the largest and most powerful republic in the Soviet Union. Freedom was limited in the Soviet Union, and religions were suppressed. Many people who lived in the Soviet Union were unhappy with Communist rule. The Soviet Union began to crumble in 1989 as republics began to break away.

Read the second paragraph. Point out that students will use their prior experience as they read the diary in this lesson.

Have volunteers read the third paragraph. Ask them to write on the first line the place or time they are recalling. Then they should list several things they remember that were different from what they were used to.

Preview the Reading Have students read the directions and preview the selection. Ask what the two photos tell about Raimonda's diary topic.

"No Words to Say Good-bye" Have students read the selection silently. Be sure students use the Check-ins to help them use their prior experience. Also be sure they read the definitions of difficult words. Encourage students to mark the text, as active readers do. At the end of the selection, have them check any marks they have made.

After You Read

B. Have students refer to their answers in Before You Read as they complete the checklist.

Extending the Reading Bring in or have students bring in diaries that interest them. Libraries have diaries from various periods in history (e.g., *The Diary of Anne Frank*) and from other lands and cultures. Encourage students to read and discuss their choices.

Think About It: Make Inferences Remind students that they worked with inferences in Lesson 4. Ask them to read the introduction.

A. 1–2. Read the first paragraph. Then have students close their books as you read each numbered paragraph and excerpt. Ask them to try to infer the answers before you read the answers given.

B. Have students do the Practice independently. Discuss their answers.

Talk About It Encourage students to talk with immigrants about these questions to get their point of view. If possible, arrange for English as a Second Language (ESL) students to participate in group discussions.

Extending the Skill Select a high-interest short story, novel, or biography. Read a passage aloud to students, stopping to ask questions that require inference. As students answer the questions, ask, *"What clues helped you fill in the missing pieces?"*

More Practice *Voyager 5 Workbook* p. 36

Write About It: Write a Diary Entry Have students read the first paragraph.

A. Read the directions, and have students read the lists. Have them write the headings *What*

Happened and *My Feelings* and list as many details as they can recall. Have them number the details in the order in which they will write about them.

B. Explain that students may write the diary in the present tense (as if writing on the day of the event) or in the past tense (looking back at the event). Encourage them to add descriptive details. Have students put their dated diary entries in their working folders.

Life Skill: Read a Schedule Have students read the explanatory material and study the schedule. Ask, *"What are the column headings?"* (Days, Times, Room, Instructor) *"What times are ABE classes taught on Mondays and Wednesdays?"* (2:30–4:30 P.M.) Be sure students can read the schedule correctly before they go on.

Practice Have students do the exercise on their own. Discuss the answers.

Extending the Life Skill Bring in multiple copies of schedules, such as bus schedules, TV or movie schedules, etc. Ask a few questions about the information shown on the schedules. Then have students work in pairs: one student asks questions about the schedule, and the other finds the answer.

Progress Evaluation Have students fill in copies of PCM 9 to include in their working folders.

Lesson 12 (p. 128)

Learning Goals Discuss the learning goals.

Before You Read Have students read the first two paragraphs. Discuss what they know about the topic of the essay.

Point out that students will use the strategy of setting a purpose as they read the essay. Have them read the third paragraph. Help them set a purpose by asking, *"What might a Chinese American woman have to share that you might learn or would like to know?"*

Have students use PCM 1 to help them set a purpose for reading. Ask students to fill in column 1 with any information they have about how it feels

to be torn between two cultures. In column 2, have them write their purpose—what they want to learn from this reading. In column 3, they can write, "Read the essay in Lesson 12." Tell students they will fill in column 4 after they have read the essay.

Preview the Reading Have students read the directions and preview the selection.

"The Struggle to Be an All-American Girl" Have students read the selection silently. Be sure they use the Check-ins to help them apply the strategy of setting a purpose. Encourage students to mark the text, as active readers do. At the end of the selection, have them check any marks they have made. Have a dictionary handy so that students can look up unfamiliar words (e.g., *dissuade, raunchy, gibberish,* and *pidgin*). Discuss how context clues could help a reader determine their meanings.

"Where Immigrants Come From" After students complete the Final Check-in, read this material with them. Point out that the chart features only a few countries, but that immigrants come to the U.S. from all over the world. Help them read the chart. Ask, *"In the 1970s, how many people came to the U.S. from China?"* (203,000) *"How many came in 1993?"* (80,000) Tell students they will work more closely with charts later in this lesson.

After You Read

B. If students created a KWHL chart before reading the selection, have them complete column 4 now.

C. Ask if students know any families in which the children teach their parents about U.S. life. If so, have them discuss the dynamics of that family.

Extending the Reading Poll the class to determine the countries or areas of the world from which students' families or ancestors came to the United States, and make a table on the board. Invite students to share stories of their families coming to the U.S., of different generations trying to adapt to life in a different culture, or of immigrants trying to live within two cultures.

Think About It: Identify the Main Idea and Details Have students read the explanatory material.

Discuss any questions they may have. Emphasize that some paragraphs have topic sentences and some don't. Tell students that if a paragraph is well-written, readers can infer the main idea even if there is no topic sentence.

A. Have students close their books. Read the paragraph and excerpt, and ask students to write the main idea. Then read the main idea underlined in the text and discuss. Have volunteers read the next two paragraphs and the excerpt. Ask students to state the main idea of the excerpt.

B. Have students do the Practice. Discuss their answers.

Talk About It Remind students that a summary is a brief retelling of the main points of a reading. Suggest that they write down the main points before giving their summaries. Encourage partners to give constructive criticism.

Extending the Skill Have students read a human interest article or essay. (Lifestyle sections of the newspaper often have readable human interest stories.) Have students use PCM 2 to identify the main idea and supporting details. Discuss the organizers with them when they are finished. Have them date their organizers and put them in their working folders.

More Practice *Voyager 5 Workbook* p. 37

Write About It: Write an Essay About a Struggle
Read the first paragraph aloud.

A. Remind students that their topic sentence should state the topic of the entire piece.

B. Remind students that it is important to state both sides of an issue, so they should be careful to explain the opposing point of view as well as their own side. Have students date their essays and put them in their working folders.

Life Skill: A Closer Look at Reading a Chart Have students read the explanatory paragraphs. Go over the chart, and ask two or three questions to be sure they understand how to read it.

Practice Let students do the exercise alone or in pairs. Have them check their answers in the Answer Key.

Extending the Life Skill If your school or program has a large ESL population, have your students research the number of ESL students and what countries they come from. Have them compile the data and organize it in a chart.

Progress Evaluation Have students fill in copies of PCM 9 to include in their working folders.

Writing Skills Mini-Lesson: Combining Ideas (p. 138)

Read the first paragraph. Explain that writing one short sentence after another can result in a choppy, disconnected writing style. Combining ideas results in more sophisticated writing.

1. Read the explanation and the examples. Be sure students know the meaning of *subject* and *verb*. Provide additional simple sentences, and ask students to combine them as shown.

2. Read rule 2. Emphasize that the meaning of the sentences determines which connecting word to use.

Practice Read the completed sentences to be sure students combined the ideas appropriately. Have students date their sentences and put them in their working folders.

More Practice *Voyager 5 Workbook* pp. 39 and 43

Unit 4 Review (p. 139)

Follow the process described in Unit 1. When students get to the editing stage of the writing process, remind them to find and fix errors in capitalization, subject-verb agreement, and sentence combining. Refer them to the Reference Handbook on pages 156–159 of *Voyager 5*.

More Practice *Voyager 5 Workbook* p. 40

Extending the Theme Use PCM 6 to extend the theme "Many Cultures." Ask students to work alone or in pairs and research a culture they are interested in. They can simply do interviews, or they can do more in-depth library research. Encourage them to learn about the culture's main language, religion, holidays, foods, and other customs. Then have them complete the grid to compare and contrast this culture with their own.

Final Note Review with students the copies of PCM 9 that they have completed for this unit. Ask what additional help they think they need with material from the three lessons and the Writing Skills Mini-Lesson in Unit 4. Discuss possible ways of meeting those needs.

Post-Assessment

When students have completed Unit 4, have them complete the Skills Review and Student Self-Assessment #2 found at the end of *Voyager 5*. (See Using the Skills Review on page 16 and Using the Student Self-Assessments on page 15.) Encourage them to evaluate their own reading and writing progress by comparing their answers to those they gave before beginning *Voyager 5*.

Alternative Assessment Follow the directions on PCM 10: Tips for Preparing a Progress Portfolio to help students evaluate the material in their working folders and assemble their progress portfolios. Then use PCM 11: Portfolio Conference Question- naire as you conduct one-on-one evaluation conferences with students.

Voyager 6 Teacher's Notes

Pre-Assessment

Before you begin Unit 1 with students, have them complete the Student Self-Assessment and the Skills Preview at the beginning of *Voyager 6* (see Using the Student Self-Assessments, page 15, and Using the Skills Preview, page 15).

In addition to *Voyager 6*, students will need
- folders in which to keep their finished work and their work in progress (see Working Folders on page 7)
- a spiral-bound or three-ring notebook to use as a personal dictionary (see Personal Dictionaries on page 18)
- a spiral-bound or three-ring notebook to use as a personal spelling list (see page 20)

▶ Unit 1: Success at Work

Part of Unit	Voyager 6 pages	TRG pages	Workbook pages
Overview	13	64 – 65	
Lesson 1	14 – 23	65 – 66	4 – 5
Lesson 2	24 – 31	66 – 67	6
Lesson 3	32 – 41	67 – 68	7 – 8
Writing Skills Mini-Lesson	42	68 – 69	9
Unit 1 Review	43 – 44	69	10 – 13

Student Objectives

Reading
- Read a personal account, job performance evaluations, and an article and bar graph.
- Apply the reading strategies of empathizing, using prior experience, and skimming.
- Understand cause and effect, identify facts and opinions, and identify the main idea and details.

Writing
- Write an explanation, a performance evaluation, and a business letter.

Speaking and Listening
- Summarize, role-play, and discuss.

Life Skill
- Read a paycheck stub, fill in a vacation request form, and read a bar graph.

▶ Unit 1 PCMs
PCM 2: Main Idea and Details Organizer
PCM 5: Cause-and-Effect Chart
PCM 8: Strategies for Recognizing Words
PCM 9: Student Progress Tracking Sheet

▶ Personal Dictionaries and Spelling Lists
Encourage students to add words they would like to learn to their dictionaries and spelling lists during each lesson in Unit 1.

▶ Word Recognition Strategies
If students need practice with recognizing words at any time, distribute copies of PCM 8 for them to work with.

Unit 1 Overview (p. 13)

This overview introduces the theme "Success at Work" and encourages students to relate to it personally before they begin Lesson 1. Call attention to the art, and discuss how it relates to the theme. Read the overview to students, or ask for volunteers to read it aloud. Discuss the question in the last paragraph. Encourage students to think about qualities they have seen in the workplace.

Be an Active Reader Explain that experienced readers are "active" readers—they think about the information as they read, and they try to figure out words and ideas they don't understand. Encourage students to mark things they don't understand. Tell them they will return to any marks they make after they have finished reading the entire selection.

Lesson 1 (p. 14)

Learning Goals Discuss the learning goals. Explain that Lesson 1 will focus on these goals.

Before You Read Read the first paragraph aloud. Point out that students will use the strategy of empathizing as they read the personal account. Explain that experienced readers try to imagine themselves in the place of people they read about to understand their feelings. Read the second paragraph and the activity. Encourage students to imagine themselves in each person's shoes as they complete the exercise. Discuss their responses.

Preview the Reading Read this section aloud, and demonstrate how to preview a reading. Look at the illustrations and ask, *"What seems to be going on in this picture? How do the two women seem to feel? What is going on in the third picture?"* Discuss with students the questions in the student book.

Use the Strategy In Before You Read, students began working with a reading strategy. Use the Strategy encourages students to apply this strategy as they read. Check-ins within the reading selection also remind students to apply the strategy as they read. Tell students to think about the question as they read the selection.

"The Deli" Explain how to use the footnotes to learn the meaning of selected words. Have students read the selection silently. Be sure they use the Check-ins to help them apply the strategy of empathizing. Encourage students to mark the text as explained in Be an Active Reader on page 13 of *Voyager 6.* At the end of the selection, have them check any marks they have made to see if they understand those parts now.

If students have underlined unfamiliar words and are unable to figure them out using PCM 8, encourage them to use a dictionary.

If students need help using a dictionary, demonstrate how. Then give them practice in looking up

words, using the pronunciation guide, and determining which definition applies.

After You Read

A. Have students do this exercise independently and check their answers in the Answer Key. Discuss any inappropriate answers. To improve reading comprehension, help students find evidence for the correct answer in the selection.

B. Discuss personal qualities that may help build empathy. Ask, *"Do you think people who show empathy are usually optimistic and naive? Or can our life experiences help us to empathize with others? Why do you feel this way?"*

C. Have students discuss the questions in pairs or small groups. If time allows, have students share their answers with the entire group. If students answer these questions in writing, encourage them to write in a personal or dialogue journal. (See Working with Adult Student Writers, page 19.)

Extending the Reading Ask students to work in pairs. Have pairs choose a thriving local business, large or small, and analyze why that business is successful. Their analyses can be based on personal observation or on interviews with customers or business owners. Have them consider these areas as they do their analyses: type of product or service; price; quality; location and business hours; competition; and customer service.

Ask them to compile their observations to answer the question "Why is this business successful?" Have volunteers present their analyses to the group.

Think About It: Understand Cause and Effect Read the introductory paragraph. On the board, draw a few cause-and-effect boxes with arrows like the ones in the student book. Fill in the boxes with simple examples of cause-and-effect relationships:

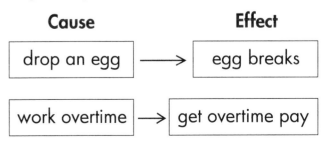

Cause		Effect
drop an egg	⟶	egg breaks
work overtime	⟶	get overtime pay

Ask students to give some everyday cause-and-effect examples as well. Make sure their examples are truly cause and effect, and not sequence of events (e.g., cook an egg → eat it; work overtime → go home).

A. Read this section as students follow along silently. As you discuss the second example, explain that inferring means to read between the lines for information that is not stated directly.

B. Have students do the Practice independently. Discuss their answers.

Talk About It Encourage group members to write down their parts of the summary. You might want to ask one member of each group to observe and evaluate whether the members' summaries, taken together, summarize the entire selection.

Extending the Skill Discuss how writers may use signal words to show cause and effect. On the board, draw cause-and-effect boxes with an arrow between them. Write an example of everyday cause and effect in the boxes (e.g., the car ran out of gas → the car stopped). Write *because* before the cause box. Under the arrow, list these signal words: *so, as a result, consequently, therefore*. Have volunteers use different signal words as they read the cause-and-effect relationship aloud. Distribute copies of PCM 5, and have students work in pairs to fill in several common cause-and-effect relationships, such as "Because the oven was too hot, the food burned," or "The alarm went off, so I woke up." Remind students to write *because* before the cause box or a signal word between the cause-and-effect boxes for each one.

More Practice *Voyager 6 Workbook* p. 4. The workbook exercises are designed to be done independently. They should not require teacher input.

Write About It: Explain How to Do Something Read the introduction aloud.

A. Have students read the directions and the example. Ask them to choose a task or activity that they know how to do well. Have them make a list like the one shown; be sure they list and number all the steps.

B. If necessary, help students write a topic sentence. Encourage them to add details as they list the steps required to do the task. Have students date their writing and put it in their working folders.

Life Skill: Read a Paycheck Stub Read the first paragraph. Ask, *"Why is it important to read the information on your paycheck stub?"* (to check that the information is accurate; to keep track of your taxes and other deductions) Go over Louise Twofeathers's paycheck stub with the class. Be sure students understand these formulas:
- gross amount = hourly rate × number of hours
- current net = current gross − (current taxes + other deductions)

Practice Have students do the Practice independently or in pairs. Check their answers. For extra practice with the formulas, provide different rates, hours, and deduction amounts, and have students calculate gross and net amounts.

Progress Evaluation Have students fill in copies of PCM 9 to include in their working folders.

Lesson 2 (p. 24)

Learning Goals Read and discuss the learning goals. Explain that Lesson 2 will focus on these goals.

Before You Read Point out that students will use their prior experience as they read the selection. Explain that thinking about related experiences and comparing them with the reading helps people better understand what they read.

Read the introductory paragraph. Ask students to use their experiences and observations and to list skills, actions, and attitudes that a supervisor might evaluate. Tell them to consider positive as well as negative things.

Preview the Reading Have students read the directions and preview the forms and the art.

Use the Strategy See Lesson 1 notes.

"Evaluation Time" Ask students to read the four-paragraph description silently. Remind students to use the Check-in to help them apply the strategy of using their prior experience. Encourage them to mark the text, as active readers do. At the end of the selection, have them check any marks they have made on the text. Be sure students understand the meaning of *E, S, N,* and *U* as you go over the evaluations together.

After You Read

A. See Lesson 1 notes.

B. Remind students to think about their own experiences and observations as they answer these questions. Point out that there are no wrong answers to these questions. Discuss their responses.

C. See Lesson 1 notes. If students have not been employed, ask them to evaluate the work they do at home or at school.

Extending the Reading Bring to class performance evaluation forms used by several businesses in your area, and ask students to bring forms used by their employers. As a class, compare and contrast the forms.

Think About It: Identify Facts and Opinions Read the first paragraph. Give students two other statements to evaluate, such as "Sondra was late for work," and "Sondra should take a different route." Discuss why the first statement is a fact, the second an opinion. Ask volunteers for other examples.

Read the next paragraph. Explain that a statement like "She's good with people" is an opinion. It is one person's interpretation of what it means to be good with people.

A. Read the paragraph and the excerpt. Discuss why "works hard and does a good job," like "good with people," is an opinion.

B. Have students do the Practice independently or in pairs. Go over their answers.

Talk About It Explain that role-playing helps build students' communication skills, which can be vital to job success. If many students prefer the supervisor's role, ask, *"What are some disadvantages of being a supervisor?"* (Supervisors are held accountable for the work done by the people they supervise, deal with employee and customer problems, must make tough decisions, and so on.)

Extending the Skill Bring in newspaper and magazine advertisements. Have students identify the facts (prices, colors, sizes) and the opinions ("best sale of the year," "the right car for you").

More Practice *Voyager 6 Workbook* p. 6

Write About It: Write a Performance Evaluation Read the first paragraph.

A. Read the text and go over the form with students. If necessary, have students find definitions for such words as *objectives* and *delegates.*

B. Have students complete the chart. Encourage them to write facts as well as opinions in their comments. Have students date their evaluations and put them in their working folders.

Life Skill: Fill In a Vacation Request Form Read the first paragraph. If students are or have been employed, ask how they have requested time off.

Practice Have students do 1–3 independently. If dates conflict on question 4, ask, *"Why is it important to negotiate in situations like this?"*

Progress Evaluation Have students fill in copies of PCM 9 to include in their working folders.

Lesson 3 (p. 32)

Learning Goals Read and discuss the learning goals. Explain that Lesson 3 will focus on these goals.

Before You Read Read the paragraph, and have students do the checklist. Discuss their responses.

Preview the Reading This lesson's reading strategy, skimming, is another way to preview. Read the paragraph, and demonstrate how to skim a reading. Then discuss the questions.

Use the Strategy See Lesson 1 notes.

"How to Be Successful at Work" Have students read the selection silently. Decide if and when you want students to read aloud. Be sure students use the Check-ins to help them apply the strategy of skimming. Remind students to mark difficult vocabulary not defined in footnotes (e.g., *excel, repetitive, collating*). At the end of the selection, have them look up any words they still don't know.

"Choosing a Job with Success in Mind" Read the introduction with students, and help them study the graph. Ask such questions as, *"Which occupation is expected to grow the fastest?"* (home health aides) *"By what percent is it expected to grow?"* (about 140 percent). Discuss what a 140 percent increase in home health aide jobs means: for every 100 jobs available in 1992, there will be an *additional* 140 jobs—a total of 240—in 2005.

After You Read
A. See Lesson 1 notes.
B. Have students skim to answer the questions.
C. See Lesson 1 notes.

Extending the Reading Poll students to find out what jobs they have had and what jobs they would like. Distribute additional research data on occupations and skills, and have students determine whether jobs in various career areas are projected to grow, decline, or remain the same.

Think About It: Identify the Main Idea and Details
Read the explanatory section aloud. Remind students that in a well-written article, the main ideas are often like building blocks:

• Each paragraph has a main idea (sometimes stated in a topic sentence, as shown in the excerpt) and supporting details.
• The main ideas of all the paragraphs in a section support the main idea of that section.
• The main ideas of all the sections of an article support the main idea of the article as a whole.

Use PCM 2 to demonstrate identifying the main idea and details of the section "Some Tips on Getting Along with People."
A. Ask students to read Part A. Check that they identified the main idea of the paragraph.
B. Remind students that facts are statements that can be verified—shown to be true. Examples

illustrate a situation. Reasons explain why something has been or should be done. Have students do the Practice independently. Discuss their answers.

Talk About It Encourage students to think about acquaintances or co-workers who have especially good interpersonal skills. Ask, *"What do these people do that works well?"* Have students list behaviors that are effective.

Extending the Skill Use PCM 2. Ask students to write the main idea of "How to Be Successful at Work" (the first sentence in the article). Have them find at least four supporting details (either the headings for the first four sections or more specific details within the article). Discuss the completed PCMs with the group.

More Practice *Voyager 6 Workbook* p. 7

Write About It: Write a Business Letter Read the first paragraph. Read through the analysis of a business letter with students, pointing to the appropriate parts in the sample. Point out that the writing style is short and to the point.
A. Suggest that students look through newspaper want ads for ideas about jobs to apply for.
B. Have students follow the directions as they draft a letter. Ask them to write the letter as if they were also including a resume. Have students date their letters and put them in their working folders.

Life Skill: Another Look at Reading a Bar Graph
Read the first paragraph aloud as students follow along. Ask if they have any questions about the graph; if so, discuss.

Practice Have students work independently. Discuss their responses to question 6.

Progress Evaluation Have students fill in copies of PCM 9 to include in their working folders.

Writing Skills Mini-Lesson: Subject-Verb Agreement with *be* and *have* (p. 42)

Read the first two sentences. Write a few simple sentences on the board, and ask volunteers to name the subject and verb for each. Then read the rest of the paragraph. Explain that many people have trouble using these verbs correctly because *be* and *have* have many forms and are used often.

1–2. Read these rules with students. If students frequently use *be* in other ways (e.g., "I be," "we is," "he were," "they was"), point out that using standard forms of *be* is important in business and formal situations, as well as on the job. Have volunteers give sentences using each form correctly.

3. Read the rules and examples. Have volunteers give other sentences using each form correctly.

Practice Ask students to complete the exercise on their own. Go over the corrected paragraph with the group, discussing each agreement issue. Have students date their writing and put it in their working folders.

Note: Habits are hard to break. Students who have used nonstandard oral English for many years will need a lot of practice to replace those speech habits. Create more drill exercises for them.

More Practice *Voyager 6 Workbook* pp. 9 and 13

Unit 1 Review (p. 43)

Explain that this review will help students evaluate what they have learned in Unit 1. Give students plenty of time to complete the review.

Reading Review Have students do the Reading Review independently. Have them check their answers against the Answer Key.

Writing Process Before students begin the writing review, turn to page 159 in *Voyager 6*. Discuss the writing process. Explain that students have already completed steps 1 and 2 for each piece of writing they have done in Unit 1. Ask students to choose the draft they would like to work with further.

To give students specific direction in revising, go over the list of points to check at the bottom of the page. When students get to the editing stage of the writing process, remind them to fix any subject-verb agreement problems they find. Work with students as they revise, edit, and create a final draft.

More Practice *Voyager 6 Workbook* p. 10

Extending the Theme To extend the theme "Success at Work," draw the following continuum on the board and have students copy it onto their own paper:

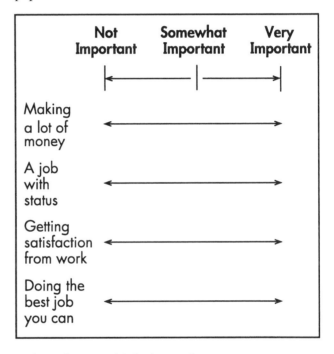

Ask students to think about what success means to them. They can add other factors if they wish. Tell them to mark the importance of each factor by placing an *X* on the appropriate spot along the continuum. Have small groups compare responses and discuss the issues. Encourage students to use their continuums to write about the theme in a paragraph titled "What Success Means to Me."

Final Note Review with students the copies of PCM 9 that they have completed for this unit. Ask what additional help they think they need with material from the three lessons and the Writing Skills Mini-Lesson in Unit 1. Discuss possible ways of meeting those needs.

► Unit 2: Taking a Stand

Part of Unit	Voyager 6 pages	TRG pages	Workbook pages
Overview	45	70	
Lesson 4	46 – 55	70 – 71	14 – 15
Lesson 5	56 – 65	71 – 72	16 – 17
Lesson 6	66 – 73	72 – 73	18
Writing Skills Mini-Lesson	74	73	19
Unit 2 Review	75 – 76	74	20 – 23

Student Objectives

Reading

- Read a story, biographical sketches, and part of a speech.
- Apply the reading strategies of using prior knowledge and predicting content.
- Identify theme, compare and contrast, and identify the main idea and details.

Writing

- Write about an incident, write a biographical sketch, and write an opinion.

Speaking and Listening

- Discuss, summarize, and read aloud.

Life Skill

- Read a political cartoon, a map, and a line graph.

► Unit 2 PCMs

PCM 1: KWHL Chart
PCM 2: Main Idea and Details Organizer
PCM 3: Story Frame
PCM 6: Comparison/Contrast Grid
PCM 7: Idea Map
PCM 8: Strategies for Recognizing Words
PCM 9: Student Progress Tracking Sheet

► Personal Dictionaries and Spelling Lists

Encourage students to add words they would like to learn to their dictionaries and spelling lists during each lesson in Unit 2.

► Word Recognition Strategies
If students need practice with recognizing words, distribute copies of PCM 8 for them to work with.

See Lesson 1 notes for lesson segments not addressed in these notes.

Unit 2 Overview (p. 45)

The overview introduces the theme "Taking a Stand" and encourages students to relate to it personally before they begin Lesson 4. Call attention to the art, and discuss how it relates to the unit theme. Have volunteers read the overview aloud. Discuss the questions in the last paragraph.

Be an Active Reader See Unit 1 notes.

Lesson 4 (p. 46)

Learning Goals Discuss the learning goals.

Before You Read Read the first paragraph. Explain that students will use their prior knowledge about certain times in U.S. history to help them understand the story in Lesson 4. Explain that experienced readers recall what they already know about a topic and use that knowledge as they read. Read the second paragraph with students, and encourage them to list things they have heard or learned about the Great Depression and how African Americans were treated at that time. Be prepared to give background information on the Ku Klux Klan if students are unfamiliar with it.

Preview the Reading Have students read the directions and preview the lesson. Discuss their predictions.

"The Right Thing to Do at the Time" Have students read the selection silently. Be sure students use the Check-ins to help them activate their prior knowledge. Encourage students to mark the text, as active readers do. At the end of the selection, have them check any marks they have made. Have volunteers read the story aloud.

After You Read

B. Ask students to give reasons to support their choice, but point out that there are no right or wrong answers for this exercise. Ask students for other suggestions. Write their ideas on the board.

Extending the Reading Have students use PCM 3 to summarize the story. Discuss their summaries.

Think About It: Identify Theme Read and discuss the explanation of theme. Be sure students can differentiate theme from topic. (Theme is the message about life; topic is the general subject.)

A. Have students read this section silently. Discuss how developing a theme is similar to supporting a main idea with details. The theme of a story is the main idea. The details of setting and action of the plot develop and support the theme.

B. Have students do the Practice independently. For question 3, ask students to skim "The Deli" if they remember it well; otherwise, have them reread it. Discuss students' answers.

Talk About It Encourage groups to list their suggestions and share them with the class.

Extending the Skill Have students read a poem or song from the Depression (e.g., "Brother, Can You Spare a Dime") or from the Civil Rights movement (e.g., "We Shall Overcome") and identify the theme.

More Practice *Voyager 6 Workbook* p. 14

Write About It: Write About an Incident

A. Read the introduction and directions. If students described a stand they made for racial equality in Talk About It, they can write about it here. Otherwise, help students choose an incident to write about. Let them know that it can seem small (e.g., insisting that a store honor its advertised prices) or large (e.g., standing up to harassment or abuse, going on strike against unfair labor practices, joining a demonstration).

B. Have students follow the directions. When students tell what happened, remind them to write the events in order. Have them date their writing and put it in their working folders.

Life Skill: Read a Political Cartoon Read the introduction together. Ask if students read political cartoons and, if so, where they find them.

Practice Read the cartoon caption. Discuss what is going on in the cartoon and how the cartoonist expresses his point of view. Have students work in pairs to complete the exercise.

Extending the Life Skill

1. Bring or have students bring political cartoons from current newspapers or magazines to discuss.
2. Have the group choose a current social or political issue. Have a brief discussion to cover some facts and opinions about the issue. Then ask students to work alone or in pairs to draw a political cartoon showing their opinion about the issue. Discuss the cartoons.

Progress Evaluation Have students fill in copies of PCM 9 to include in their working folders.

Lesson 5 (p. 56)

Learning Goals Discuss the learning goals.

Before You Read Explain that students will use the strategy of predicting content as they read this selection. Read and discuss the first two paragraphs. Then have students do the pre-reading checklist.

Discuss what students know about the struggle for human rights in other parts of the world. Explain that the women profiled in "Extraordinary People" are human rights advocates from Guatemala and Burma. Distribute copies of PCM 1. Ask students to write this topic: "The human rights struggle in Guatemala and Burma." Have them complete the first three columns of the chart. In column 3, students can list "read 'Extraordinary People,'" but they should list at least one other type of research as well.

You may want to discuss definitions of some key words in these sketches, such as *displaced, repression,* and *guerrillas,* before students begin to read.

Preview the Reading Have students read the directions and preview the selections. Find Guatemala and Burma (called Myanmar by the military government) on a world map or globe.

"Extraordinary People" Have students read the selection silently. Be sure students use the Check-ins to help them apply the strategy of using their prior knowledge. Help them pronounce proper names. Make sure they understand that *b. 1960* means "born in 1960." Encourage students to mark the text, as active readers do. At the end of both selections, have them check any marks they have made. Have volunteers read the articles aloud.

After You Read
B. Have students look back at their answers in Before You Read and add two other items.

Extending the Reading Encourage students to find out the current status of Menchú and Suu Kyi. Have volunteers report their findings. Have students complete their KWHL charts.

Think About It: Compare and Contrast Read and discuss the introductory paragraphs.
A. Read this section aloud, and go over the chart. Be sure students understand that the column headed *Both* represents a comparison.
B. Have students do the Practice in pairs or independently. Tell them to look back through the article to find answers. Check their answers.

Talk About It Ask partners to evaluate each other's summary: Were all the main points covered? Were they told in the correct sequence? Were less important details left out?

Extending the Skill Have students research a person noted for human rights work, perhaps a recent recipient of the Nobel Peace Prize. Have students find this information:
• brief biographical data
• background on the humanitarian issue
• the work the person did

Have pairs of students use PCM 6 to compare and contrast the people they researched. Ask pairs to compile the information into a brief report and make an oral presentation to the class.

More Practice *Voyager 6 Workbook* p. 16

Write About It: Write a Biographical Sketch Read the first paragraph. Help students find subjects to write about. List these ideas on the board: *family members, co-workers, bosses, ministers.* Encourage students to add others, then choose one. If students researched a famous person for Extending the Skill, they may choose to write about that person.
A. Read through the questions with students; brainstorm others with the group.
B. Tell students to include the most interesting details and information, but to cover the basics as well (e.g., age, profession, family information). Have students date their writing and put it in their working folders.

Life Skill: Read a Map Read the explanatory paragraphs. Be sure students understand how north, south, east, and west are labeled on the map.

Practice Have students complete the activity independently or as a group.

Progress Evaluation Have students fill in copies of PCM 9 to include in their working folders.

Lesson 6 (p. 66)

Learning Goals Discuss the learning goals.

Before You Read Explain that students will use their prior knowledge—information they know about Dr. King and the Civil Rights movement—to help them understand his speech "I Have a Dream." Have students list and then share details about Dr. King.

Preview the Reading Have students read the directions and preview the selection.

"I Have a Dream" Have students read the speech silently. Be sure they use the Check-ins to help them activate their prior knowledge. The quotation noted in the first Check-in is from the Declaration of Independence. The quotation beginning "every valley shall be exalted" is from the Bible, Isaiah 41:4–5. Encourage students to mark the text, as active readers do. At the end of the selection, have them check any marks they have made. Ask volunteers to read the speech aloud.

After You Read

B. Discuss students' answers, and have them give reasons to support them.

Extending the Reading Bring in the entire text of "I Have a Dream," and have students read and discuss it together. If possible, play an audio- or videotape of Dr. King delivering the speech at the 1963 March on Washington.

Think About It: Identify the Main Idea and Details

Read the first section with students. Remind them that *implied* means not stated directly.

A. Have students read the excerpt and note its main idea and details.

B. Before students complete question 1, ask, *"What is the implied main idea of this excerpt?"* (We can endure because we have faith that we will be free in the future.) Have them complete the Practice.

Talk About It Help students practice their oral reading skills before having volunteers read aloud.

Extending the Skill Use PCM 2 with another famous speech, such as Lincoln's Gettysburg Address. Help students identify the main ideas and supporting details.

More Practice *Voyager 6 Workbook* p. 18

Write About It: Write an Opinion Read and discuss the first paragraph.

A. Have students first circle *do* or *do not* in the center circle to indicate their opinion. Then ask them to write examples or reasons supporting their opinion in the ovals. Tell them to add more ovals if needed. If you prefer, you can provide students with copies of PCM 7 instead.

B. Help students decide whether to write one paragraph or several. If they use several sentences to explain each supporting detail, each detail requires a separate paragraph. Have them date their writing and put it in their working folders.

Life Skill: Read a Line Graph Read the first paragraph. Have students read the title and the labels along each axis. Be sure they understand the key. Explain that line graphs show trends at a glance— you can quickly see whether a quantity rises, falls, or stays the same over time.

Practice Have students do the Practice and check their answers.

Extending the Life Skill Ask students to bring line graphs from newspapers or magazines. Pairs of students can work together to ask and answer questions about them.

Progress Evaluation Have students fill in copies of PCM 9 to include in their working folders.

Writing Skills Mini-Lesson: Commas in Compound Sentences (p. 74)

To successfully complete this lesson, students first must understand what a simple sentence is. Give examples as needed.

1. Point out the two complete thoughts in the examples. Ask students for other examples of compound sentences. Write them on the board, and have students identify the subject and verb in each clause. Ask where the comma should be placed.

2. Ask students for other examples of sentences with compound subjects and compound verbs. Write them on the board, and point out that there is no comma.

Practice Go over students' completed paragraphs as a group.

More Practice *Voyager 6 Workbook* pp. 19 and 23

Unit 2 Review (p. 75)

Follow the process described in Unit 1. When students get to the editing stage of the Writing Process, remind them to fix any problems with subject-verb agreement and compound sentences.

More Practice *Voyager 6 Workbook* p. 20

Extending the Theme To extend the theme "Taking a Stand," read together *To Kill a Mockingbird* by Harper Lee, or watch the movie based on the book. When students have finished, have them complete PCM 3 and discuss it. Ask: *"Who took a stand? For what cause? What were the results?"* Invite students to share their feelings and reactions to the story.

Final Note Review with students the copies of PCM 9 that they have completed for this unit. Ask what additional help they think they need with material from the three lessons and the Writing Skills Mini-Lesson in Unit 2. Discuss possible ways of meeting those needs.

▶ Unit 3: Relationships

Part of Unit	Voyager 6 pages	TRG pages	Workbook pages
Overview	77	75	
Lesson 7	78 – 87	75 – 76	24 – 25
Lesson 8	88 – 97	76 – 77	26 – 27
Lesson 9	98 – 105	77 – 78	28
Writing Skills Mini-Lesson	106	78	29
Unit 3 Review	107 – 108	78 – 79	30 – 33

Student Objectives

Reading
- Read scenes from a play, a story, and bar graphs.
- Apply the reading strategies of visualizing, imagining, and using prior knowledge.
- Make inferences, identify theme, and identify facts and opinions.

Writing
- Write dialogue, a friendly letter, and an opinion.

Speaking and Listening
- Read aloud and discuss.

Life Skill
- Read a map, a family tree, and a double line graph.

▶ Unit 3 PCMs
PCM 1: KWHL Chart
PCM 3: Story Frame
PCM 7: Idea Map
PCM 8: Strategies for Recognizing Words
PCM 9: Student Progress Tracking Sheet

▶ Personal Dictionaries and Spelling Lists
Encourage students to add words they would like to learn to their dictionaries and spelling lists during each lesson in Unit 3.

▶ Word Recognition Strategies
If students need practice with recognizing words, distribute copies of PCM 8 for them to work with.

See Lesson 1 notes for lesson segments not addressed in these notes.

Unit 3 Overview (p. 77)

The overview introduces the theme "Relationships" and encourages students to relate to it personally before they begin Lesson 7. Have volunteers read the overview aloud. Discuss the questions in the last paragraph. Discuss how the art relates to the unit theme.

Be an Active Reader See Unit 1 notes.

Lesson 7 (p. 78)

Learning Goals Discuss the learning goals.

Before You Read Ask if anyone has seen the play or the movie version of *On Golden Pond*. If so, have them tell the others about it. Have students read the two lines of dialogue and answer the questions.

Explain that when we visualize, we picture in our minds what we are reading about. Because a playwright does not give detailed descriptions of characters' looks and actions, visualizing is especially necessary when reading a play.

Preview the Reading Have students read the directions and preview the selection. Ask, *"What characters speak in this scene?"*

"On Golden Pond" After students read the background information, ask, *"Who is Ethel? Who is Norman? Who is Chelsea? Where does this scene take place?"* Be sure students use the Check-ins to help them apply the strategy of visualizing. Encourage students to mark the text, as active readers do. At the end of the selection, have them check any marks they have made. Have students read the scenes aloud, taking turns playing the three parts.

After You Read
B. Ask students to jot down details they visualized. Have them share their ideas.

Extending the Reading Show the same scenes from the videotape of the movie. Ask students to compare and contrast reading a play with seeing it presented. Discuss how visualizing helps a reader understand.

Think About It: Make Inferences Discuss the introduction. Emphasize that readers often must make inferences to understand things the author does not state directly.
A. Have students read the question and excerpt and make the inference. Then read and discuss the inferences given in the text. If necessary, explain that sarcasm is a bitter type of humor often meant to hurt someone's feelings.
B. Help students answer the first question; if necessary, point out lines that help lead to inferences. Have students complete the Practice. Discuss their answers, and have them support their inferences with evidence from the excerpt.

Talk About It Have students practice reading their lines. Encourage them to use appropriate gestures and facial expressions. Ask each group to present their scenes to the class.

Extending the Skill Read *On Golden Pond*. Discuss relationships as they develop, particularly the relationship between Norman and the boy. Have students list at least three inferences they make as they read. Discuss the play and students' inferences.

More Practice *Voyager 6 Workbook* p. 24

Write About It: Write Dialogue Have students read the first paragraph. Encourage them to imagine characters and a relationship they think will be interesting. You might have the group brainstorm for topics.
A. Have students read and follow the directions. Point out that the sample word map shows the

basic ideas in order, while the dialogue is detailed and complete.
B. Encourage students to listen to their dialogue and visualize people actually saying their lines. Have them date their dialogues and put them in their working folders.

Life Skill: Read a Map Read the first paragraph with students. Point out the key and the compass. Be sure that students know that north is at the top of the map.

Practice Have students work in pairs and check their answers.

Extending the Life Skill Bring to class street maps for your community. Ask students to work in pairs to write at least three questions about the map. Have them exchange questions with another pair and write answers to each other's questions.

Progress Evaluation Have students fill in copies of PCM 9 to include in their working folders.

Lesson 8 (p. 88)

Learning Goals Discuss the learning goals.

Before You Read Read the first paragraph. Point out that students will use the strategy of imagining as they read the story. Explain that experienced readers try to imagine what the characters are thinking and feeling. Have students read the second paragraph and answer the questions. If students seem eager to discuss their responses, do so.

Preview the Reading Have students preview the selection.

"The Corn Planting" Have students read the selection silently. Be sure students use the Check-ins to help them apply the strategy of imagining. Encourage students to mark the text, as active readers do. At the end of the selection, have them check any marks they have made. Since this is a long story, you may want students to read aloud selected sections only.

After You Read
B. Encourage students to imagine Hal's feelings, and discuss why Hal blurted out the bad news.

Extending the Reading Discuss the elements of fiction: setting, characterization, plot. Have students use PCM 3 to identify these elements in "The Corn Planting."

Think About It: Identify Theme Have students read the first paragraph.
A. After students read part A, discuss the statement of the theme to make sure students understand it.
B. Have students do the Practice independently. As they read each excerpt, suggest they ask themselves, "Does this relate to life going on despite death?" Discuss their answers.

Talk About It Have students list the qualities of the couples and their relationships that seem to lead to strong, long-lasting relationships.

Extending the Skill Ask students to read a short story, and have them identify the theme. Or if students have read *To Kill a Mockingbird* or *On Golden Pond,* suggested as extension activities in previous lessons, ask them to identify the theme in one of these works.

More Practice *Voyager 6 Workbook* p. 26

Write About It: Write a Friendly Letter Have students read the first paragraph and choose the person to whom they will write.
A. Help students list ideas to write about. Tell them they can choose from their list the ideas they want to include.
B. Before students begin writing, study the format of a friendly letter. Ask students to name other words they can use as a closing (*Sincerely, Yours truly, Your friend*). Have them put their dated letters in their working folders.

Life Skill: Read a Family Tree Read the first paragraph, and discuss the sample family tree with students.

Practice Have students do this exercise in pairs. You may need to discuss terms of relationships (e.g., *grandparents, first cousins*) to help students understand the diagram and answer the questions. Go over the answers as a class.

Progress Evaluation Have students fill in copies of PCM 9 to include in their working folders.

Lesson 9 (p. 98)

Learning Goals Discuss the learning goals.

Before You Read Have students read this section. Point out that they will use their prior knowledge as they study the graphs. Briefly discuss some things they might write about family relationships.

Students may want to fill in PCM 1. If so, they might write "Read the graphs in this lesson" in the column headed *H.*

Preview the Reading Have students read the directions and preview the graphs.

"Bar Graph for Size of Households" Read and discuss the explanation with students. Point out that the vertical label ("in thousands") indicates that you must multiply each number by 1,000 to find the actual number of persons. Remind students that to multiply by 1,000, you can simply add a comma and three 0s at the end of the number. Have students practice multiplying numbers on the vertical axis by 1,000. Have volunteers take turns asking and answering other questions about the graph.

"A Double Bar Graph" Read this section with students. Point out each feature of the graph as it is described. Have students identify the year and the percents shown for the category "neither parent." Then have them study the graph and answer the questions. Discuss their answers. Read the Final Check-in, and discuss the questions.

After You Read
B. To broaden the discussion, ask, *"What are some advantages and disadvantages for children who live with one parent, both parents, or one or both grandparents?"*

If students began a KWHL chart before they read the graphs, have them complete the column headed *L* now.

Extending the Reading Have students work in groups to compile data that reflects something about relationships. They can use such sources as

Statistical Abstract of the United States or a U.S. Census Bureau publication. Help them select data that is appropriate for a bar graph. Have groups create bar graphs from the data they select. Have each group present their graphs to the other groups for discussion.

Think About It: Identify Facts and Opinions Have students read the explanatory section.
A. Discuss why each statement is a fact or an opinion.
B. Have students do the Practice independently. Remind them to ask "Can this be proved true by the data on the graph?" as they evaluate each statement. Discuss their answers.

Talk About It Encourage students to read these questions carefully and think about them before they discuss them.

Extending the Skill Ask each student to write three facts and three opinions about politics, religion, or lifestyles. Have students exchange statements with a partner and identify which statements are facts and which are opinions.

More Practice *Voyager 6 Workbook* p. 28

Write About It: Write Your Opinion Read the first paragraph.
A. Help students choose a topic pertaining to relationships. List on the board broad areas (dating, marriage, divorce, parenthood, families, relatives, friendship). Have them consider how they feel about the topic they choose and write an opinion statement expressing their feelings. Next, ask them to list several reasons supporting or explaining their opinion. Encourage them to list facts and examples rather than other opinions. You may want to distribute copies of PCM 7 to help students generate and organize their ideas.
B. Students should follow the directions. Have them date their writing and put it in their working folders.

Life Skill: Read a Double Line Graph Read the first paragraph with students. Have students identify the title, the labels, and the key. Be sure students recognize the different lines used to show marriages

and divorces. Review the concept "rate per 1,000 population": 9.1 out of every 1,000 people got married in 1994; 4.6 out of every 1,000 people got divorced in 1994.

Practice Have students work alone or in pairs. Discuss their responses.

Progress Evaluation Have students fill in copies of PCM 9 to include in their working folders.

Writing Skills Mini-Lesson: Writing Complex Sentences (p. 106)

Begin the lesson by reviewing compound sentences (in the Writing Skills Mini-Lesson in Unit 2). Then read and discuss the first section with students. Be sure students understand that "when I worked at Pizza World" is not a complete thought. Write other examples of complex sentences on the board, and have students identify the independent and dependent clauses.
1. Read the explanation and the examples. Using the example sentences you wrote, ask students to reverse the placement of the clauses and to point out where a comma should be placed.
2. Point out that the connecting word is the word that begins the dependent clause. Use several of the connecting words in complex sentences. Ask students to give example sentences as well.

Practice Ask students to exchange their completed sentences with a partner. Have partners read the sentences and correct them together. Have students date their writing and put it in their working folders.

More Practice *Voyager 6 Workbook* pp. 29 and 33

Unit 3 Review (p. 107)

See Unit 1 notes. When students get to the editing stage of the writing process, remind them to fix any problems they find with subject-verb agreement or compound and complex sentences.

More Practice *Voyager 6 Workbook* p. 30

Extending the Theme To extend the theme "Relationships," ask students to think about their relationship with another person who is very important to them. Ask them to express their feelings about this relationship in some way. They can express their feelings by writing a paragraph, a poem, or a story; drawing or painting a picture; making a sculpture or collage; or creating a cartoon. Ask volunteers to present and explain their projects to the class. If possible, provide space to display their projects.

Final Note Review with students the copies of PCM 9 that they have completed for this unit. Ask what additional help they think they need with material from the three lessons and the Writing Skills Mini-Lesson in Unit 3. Discuss possible ways of meeting those needs.

▶ Unit 4: Insights

Part of Unit	Voyager 6 pages	TRG pages	Workbook pages
Overview	109	80	
Lesson 10	110 – 119	80 – 81	34 – 35
Lesson 11	120 – 127	81 – 82	36 – 37
Lesson 12	128 – 137	82 – 84	38
Writing Skills Mini-Lesson	138	84	39
Unit 4 Review	139 – 140	84	40 – 43

Student Objectives

Reading
- Read an autobiography, a personal account, and a biographical article.
- Apply the reading strategies of imagining, empathizing, and using prior experience.
- Make inferences, compare and contrast, and understand cause and effect.

Writing
- Write the results of an interview, compare and contrast two things, and write a cause-and-effect paragraph.

Speaking and Listening
- Discuss and tell a story.

Life Skill
- Read a time line, fill in a hospital admission form, and read a circle graph.

▶ Unit 4 PCMs
PCM 5: Cause-and-Effect Chart
PCM 6: Comparison/Contrast Grid
PCM 7: Idea Map
PCM 8: Strategies for Recognizing Words
PCM 9: Student Progress Tracking Sheet

▶ Personal Dictionaries and Spelling Lists
Encourage students to add words they would like to learn to their dictionaries and spelling lists during each lesson in Unit 4.

▶ Word Recognition Strategies
If students need practice with recognizing words, distribute copies of PCM 8 for them to work with.

See **Lesson 1 notes** for lesson segments not addressed in these notes.

Unit 4 Overview (p. 109)

The overview introduces the theme "Insights" and encourages students to relate to it personally before they begin Lesson 10. Have volunteers read the overview aloud. Call attention to the art, and discuss how it relates to the unit theme. Discuss the questions, and encourage students to give examples of times when they have had an insight.

Be an Active Reader See Unit 1 notes.

Lesson 10 (p. 110)

Learning Goals Discuss the learning goals.

Before You Read Read the introduction. Explain that a biography is someone's life story written by another person. When you write your own life story, it is called an autobiography. Point out that students will use the strategy of imagining as they read the autobiography in this lesson.

Talk about the different modes we use to communicate: spoken and written words, sign language, facial expressions, and body language. Discuss what happens when two people do not share the same mode. Next, emphasize that at the beginning of this narrative, Keller cannot see, hear, or speak. Ask, *"If you could not hear or see, how would you learn to talk? Would you know you were making sounds when you yelled or cried?"* Have volunteers try to move around the room blindfolded.

Preview the Reading Have students read the directions and preview the selection.

"The Story of My Life" Point out the year in which the events take place (1887), and explain that Keller's writing—word choice, tone, sentence structure—reflects a style used by writers in the late 19th century. You may want to read the excerpt to students to help them understand the difficult syntax. Then have them reread it silently. Be sure they use the Check-ins to help them apply the strategy of imagining. Encourage them to mark the text, as active readers do. At the end of the selection, have them check any marks they have made.

After You Read

B. Encourage students to add other adjectives to describe how they might feel.

Extending the Reading Show a videotape of the movie *The Miracle Worker,* which tells the story of Helen Keller and Anne Sullivan. If you can't show the whole film, show the climax, where Helen suddenly understands the relationship between water itself and the word *water.*

Think About It: Make Inferences

A. Have students read this section and try to make the inference themselves before reading the answer. Discuss the inference.

B. Work through the first question with students. Point out that the key phrase is "when she wrote this." Have students complete 2–4 independently, and discuss their responses. Have them support their inferences.

Talk About It Point out that medical and educational resources are much more advanced today than they were in the 1880s. Ask students to consider how they would feel and how they would use modern resources if confronted with this problem.

Extending the Skill Have students reread the selection and note references to Helen's teacher, Anne Sullivan. Then ask them to make inferences about her and support their inferences with evidence from the selection. For example, we may infer that Anne Sullivan was persistent from the sentence, "In despair she had dropped the subject for the time, only to renew it at the first opportunity."

More Practice *Voyager 6 Workbook* p. 34

Write About It: Write the Results of an Interview Have students read the first paragraph.

A. Have students read this section and write more questions if they would like. Tell students that they will probably need to explain what they mean by *insight* to the person they interview. Remind them to take notes on the responses.

B. Remind students to write a detailed descriptive paragraph. Have students date their paragraphs and put them in their working folders.

Life Skill: Read a Time Line Read the first paragraph and study the first time line with students. Point out that events are listed in time order from left to right. Let students read the second time line on their own.

Practice Have students do the Practice independently. Discuss their answers.

Progress Evaluation Have students fill in copies of PCM 9 to include in their working folders.

Lesson 11 (p. 120)

Learning Goals Discuss the learning goals.

Before You Read Point out that students will use the strategy of empathizing to help them understand the feelings and motivations of the people they read about in this lesson. Have students read this section and do the exercise independently. Discuss their answers.

Preview the Reading Have students read the directions and preview the selection. Have them jot down their predictions.

"A Fear I Had" Have students read the selection silently. Be sure they use the Check-ins to help them apply the strategy of empathizing. Encourage them to mark the text, as active readers do. At the end of the selection, have them check any marks they have made. Also have them compare their preview predictions with the actual cause of the author's fear.

After You Read

B. Ask students to put themselves in Zoraida's place as they answer these questions.

Extending the Reading Write the quotation "The Child is father of the Man" on the board. Discuss how events that happen in childhood can affect us as adults. You may prompt students by writing several topics on the board, such as *school, men, women, parenting, authority, home, work,* and *outside pressures.* Discuss how attitudes toward any of these topics are shaped by what happened in the past. Students may find it helpful to use PCM 5 in tracking and organizing their thoughts.

Think About It: Compare and Contrast

A. Have students read this section and study the chart. Discuss any questions they have.

B. You may want to help students with the first chart. Discuss how "a typical mother" is a subjective notion. There are no right or wrong answers for that column in the first chart. Then have students complete both charts independently. Discuss their answers.

Talk About It These emotionally charged situations may cause heated discussions. You may need to remind students to respect others' opinions.

Extending the Skill Have students think of an insight they had. Tell them to think about what things changed and what remained the same. Have them use PCM 6 to compare and contrast elements in their life before and after having the insight. They can label column 2 *Before* and column 3 *After.*

More Practice *Voyager 6 Workbook* p. 36

Write About It: Compare and Contrast Two Things

Have students read the first paragraph.

A. Encourage students to choose a subject that has many different features to compare and contrast. Students can use PCM 6 to help them organize their ideas.

B. Encourage students to write four paragraphs— one for each of the numbered steps. Each paragraph should have a main idea sentence and two or more detail sentences.

  1. The opening paragraph introduces the subject (e.g., "I've had several jobs. My most recent jobs were waiting tables and detailing cars.").

  2. The second paragraph lists similarities between the two examples.

3. The third paragraph lists differences.

4. The concluding paragraph can state a preference (e.g., "I prefer waiting tables to detailing cars. I liked the noisy atmosphere full of people, and I liked earning tips.").

Have students date their writing and put it in their working folders.

Life Skill: Fill In a Hospital Admission Form Have students read the first paragraph and look over the sample form. If necessary, explain terms students don't know (e.g., *referring physician, type of plan, all charges incurred*).

Practice Students can fill in the form using their own information, or they can make up information if they prefer.

Progress Evaluation Have students fill in copies of PCM 9 to include in their working folders.

Lesson 12 (p. 128)

Learning Goals Discuss the learning goals.

Before You Read Have students read the first paragraph. Point out that they will use their prior experience as they read the biographical article in this lesson. Have them read the second paragraph and complete the pre-reading activity. Help them list skills by asking, *"What are some things you do at work? To enjoy yourself? To help your family?"*

Preview the Reading Have students read the directions and preview the selection. Discuss the questions.

"A Success as a Teacher and Builder, John Corcoran Had a Humiliating Secret: He Couldn't Read or Write" Have students read the selection silently. Be sure they use the Check-ins to help them use their prior experience. Encourage them to mark the text, as active readers do. At the end of the selection, have them check any marks they have made. Ask volunteers to read selected sections aloud.

After You Read

B. Remind students to think of their own experience—not Corcoran's—as they evaluate these statements.

Extending the Reading Discuss the authors' lively, descriptive style in the article. Point out three techniques used in the article and examples from the first two paragraphs:

1. Quotes, which help readers get to know people's thoughts and feelings (e.g., "If the truth got out, how could I support my family? So my life turned into a nightmare.")
2. Interesting verb choices (e.g., success *sat;* he *sported*)
3. Figurative comparisons (e.g., a speaking voice that played bass fiddle on a listener's bones, and ice-blue eyes that lit up like headlights)

Ask students to find at least two other interesting verbs and at least three other figurative comparisons in the article. Then ask, *"If the authors had not used these descriptive techniques, would you have gotten as clear a picture of Corcoran and his problem? Why or why not?"*

Think About It: Understand Cause-and-Effect Chains
Have students read the first paragraph. If necessary, review basic cause-and-effect relationships.
A. Have students fill in the missing elements in the chain. Discuss their responses, and compare them with the answers given in the text.
B. Have students do the Practice independently. Discuss their answers.

Talk About It Discuss briefly the importance of reading and telling stories to children. Discuss stories that students might read or tell to a young child. Encourage them to do so and to report on how successful the storytelling was.

Extending the Skill Use PCM 5. Ask students to identify other cause-and-effect sequences in Corcoran's life, such as:

1. As an adult in the business world:
   couldn't read → worried he'd lose his job
   worried he'd lose his job → lived like a fugitive
2. As a teacher:
   couldn't read or write → no written assignments
   no written assignments → students learned in other ways
3. Effects on his personal relationships:
   afraid of being exposed → kept people away

kept people away → had few friends
had few friends → terribly lonely at times

Have students date their charts and put them in their working folders.

More Practice *Voyager 6 Workbook* p. 38

Write About It: Write a Cause-and-Effect Paragraph
Have students read the first section silently.
A. Help students choose a topic. Remind them that insights do not always occur suddenly. Write the following topics on the board:

An insight into
• the underlying cause of a problem
• the reason something happened
• how to do something you couldn't before
• how to handle a tough situation

Have students brainstorm more topics. Then ask each student to select one. Distribute copies of PCM 5, and have students jot down causes and effects leading to and resulting from the insight they chose.

B. Have students follow the directions. If it takes three or more sentences to state the problem, have students write two paragraphs: one describing the problem, the other describing the insight and the results from having the insight. Have students date their writing and put it in their working folders.

Life Skill: Read a Circle Graph Read and discuss the explanation with students. Be sure they understand that 100 percent means the total amount (e.g., 100 percent of a population means the entire population). Look at the graph with students. Ask, *"What do all of these percents add up to?"* (100 percent). Point out that the asterisk indicates a footnote at the bottom of the graph.

Practice Have students do this exercise alone or in pairs.

Extending the Life Skill Have students compile data and make a circle graph as a class. Let them decide the subject of the graph and conduct research to gather data. Discuss how to convert the data into percentages by dividing each part by the whole. If students' data doesn't total 100 percent, discuss using a category labeled *Other.*

Progress Evaluation Have students fill in copies of PCM 9 to include in their working folders.

Writing Skills Mini-Lesson: Correcting Pronoun Problems (p. 138)

Review the definition of a noun: a word indicating a person *(father, Aunt Betty, Dr. Jones)*, place *(Cincinnati, downtown, home)*, or thing *(car, leaf, refrigerator)*. Have students give other examples of each.

Read the first paragraph and the examples. Point out that *She* is the subject of the sentence.

1. Read the explanation and the examples. Ask students for examples of other sentences that use subject pronouns. Have them also identify the verbs.

2. Read the explanation and the examples. Have students identify the subjects, verbs, and objects. Explain that the subject does something to, for, or with an object (e.g., He found me. She took them home. We gave it to him.). Give other examples of sentences with object pronouns; have students identify the pronouns and the verbs. Have students give other examples as well.

3. Read the explanation. Note that people often misuse compound subject pronouns. Point out that *I* is most frequently misused. Read the examples as two separate sentences: "My mother talked to her." "My mother talked to me." Ask: *"Would you say 'My mother talked to she' or 'My mother talked to I'? Then you shouldn't say, 'My mother talked to she and I' or 'My mother talked to her and I.'"*

Practice Read students' completed sentences together. Have students practice separating compound pronouns as described above. Have students date their writing and put it in their working folders.

More Practice *Voyager 6 Workbook* pp. 39 and 43

Unit 4 Review (p. 139)

Follow the process described in Unit 1. When students get to the editing stage of the writing process, remind them to fix any problems they find with subject-verb agreement, compound and complex sentences, and pronouns.

More Practice *Voyager 6 Workbook* p. 40

Extending the Theme To extend the theme "Insights," discuss how students have seen that insights can come from formal education or life experience. Ask students to think of the insights they have gained through education and experience. Did the insights come all at once or over a period of time? Is one kind of insight more valuable than the other? Have students write their opinions about insights. Distribute copies of PCM 7 for them to use in generating and organizing their ideas. Remind them to include specific details and examples.

Final Note Review with students the copies of PCM 9 that they have completed for this unit. Ask what additional help they think they need with material from the three lessons and the Writing Skills Mini-Lesson in Unit 4. Discuss possible ways of meeting those needs.

Post-Assessment

When students have completed Unit 4, be sure they complete the Skills Review and Student Self-Assessment #2 found at the end of *Voyager 6*. (See Using the Skills Review on page 16 and Using the Student Self-Assessments on page 15.) Encourage them to evaluate their own reading and writing progress by comparing their answers to those they gave before beginning *Voyager 6*.

Alternative Assessment Follow the directions on PCM 10: Tips for Preparing a Progress Portfolio to help students evaluate the material in their working folders and assemble their progress portfolios. Then use PCM 11: Portfolio Conference Questionnaire as you conduct one-on-one evaluation conferences with students.

Photocopy Masters

The following photocopy masters (PCMs) can be photocopied for classroom activities and homework. Here are brief suggestions for using each PCM.

▶ **PCM 1: KWHL Chart** Use this PCM as described in the lesson notes to prepare for reading. It helps students identify what they know about a topic, what they want to learn, and how they plan to learn it. It also helps students identify what they learned about the topic after reading. (Can use with *Voyager 4*, Lesson 2 and Units 1 and 2, Extending the Theme; *Voyager 5*, Lessons 1 and 12; *Voyager 6*, Lessons 5 and 9.)

▶ **PCM 2: Main Idea and Details Organizer** Use this PCM as described in the lesson notes to give students extra practice in identifying the main idea and details in what they read. (Can use with *Voyager 4*, Lessons 4, 6, and 11; *Voyager 5*, Lessons 1 and 12; *Voyager 6*, Lessons 3 and 6.)

▶ **PCM 3: Story Frame** Use this PCM as described in the lesson notes to help students summarize the setting, plot, and characterization in a piece of fiction. (Can use whenever students read fiction or prepare to retell a story; specifically with *Voyager 6*, Lessons 4 and 8, and Unit 2, Extending the Theme.)

▶ **PCM 4: Problem/Solution Work Sheet** Use this PCM as described in the lesson notes to help students recognize problems and solutions in reading selections. Used as a prewriting tool, it can also help students identify the cause(s) of a problem, determine possible solutions, evaluate the solutions, and choose the best one. (Can use with *Voyager 4*, Lessons 1 and 7; *Voyager 5*, Lessons 3, 6, and 9.)

▶ **PCM 5: Cause-and-Effect Chart** Use this PCM as described in the lesson notes to help students identify cause-and-effect relationships. It can be used to analyze single cause-and-effect relationships or a cause-and-effect chain of events. (Can use with *Voyager 4*, Lessons 3 and 4; *Voyager 6*, Lessons 1, 11, and 12.)

▶ **PCM 6: Comparison/Contrast Grid** Use this PCM as described in the lesson notes to help students compare and contrast information found in a reading. Used as a prewriting tool, it can also help students organize information for a compare/contrast piece. (Can use with *Voyager 5*, Lesson 10, and Unit 4, Extending the Theme; *Voyager 6*, Lessons 5 and 11.)

▶ **PCM 7: Idea Map** Use this PCM as a prewriting tool as described in the lesson notes. It helps students organize and support their opinion about a topic. (Can use with *Voyager 4*, Lessons 10 and 11; *Voyager 5*, Lesson 9; *Voyager 6*, Lessons 6 and 9, and Unit 4, Extending the Theme.)

▶ **PCM 8: Strategies for Recognizing Words** Use this PCM whenever students need practice with decoding skills. It gives them strategies for decoding unknown words.

▶ **PCM 9: Student Progress Tracking Sheet** Have students complete this PCM each time they finish a lesson. It will help them reflect on what they learned in the lesson.

▶ **PCM 10: Tips for Preparing a Progress Portfolio** Use this PCM as a guide to help students prepare their portfolios. Preparing a portfolio may take quite a while. Discuss each question and option with students. Encourage students to evaluate each option carefully. Be sure they consider the questions on PCM 11 before you schedule a portfolio conference.

▶ **PCM 11: Portfolio Conference Questionnaire** When students have assembled their portfolios, schedule individual conferences. Ask the questions on PCM 11. Discuss the student's answers. Emphasize the progress the student has shown, using the samples chosen for the portfolio.

KWHL Chart

Before you begin reading, write the topic of the reading selection on the line. Then complete the first three columns on the chart (the *K*, *W*, and *H* columns). After you finish reading the selection, complete the fourth column.

My Topic _____

K What I Already Know About This Topic	W What I Want to Learn About This Topic	H How I Will Learn It	L What I Learned About This Topic

Main Idea and Details Organizer

The **main idea** of a piece of writing is the most important point that the writer wants to share. **Supporting details** give more information about the main idea.

Write the main idea of a writing selection on the line below. Then write details that support the main idea.

Main Idea

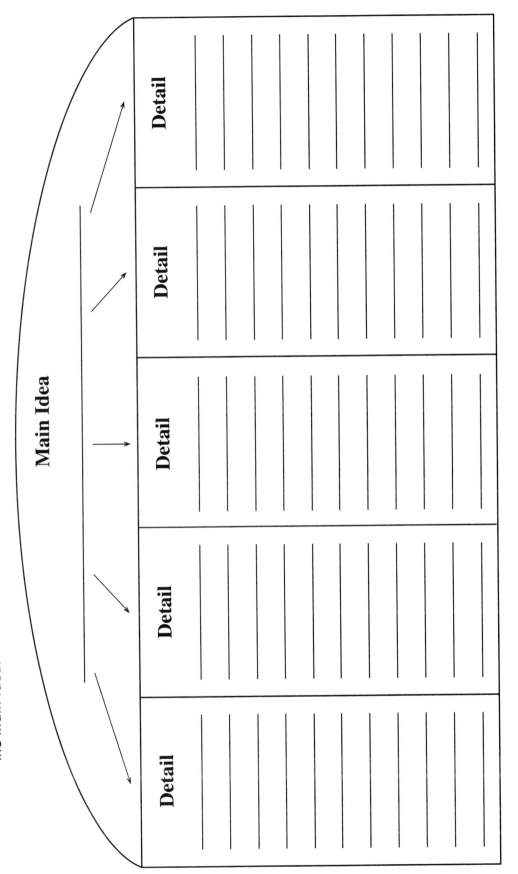

Detail	Detail	Detail	Detail	Detail

Story Frame

Title _____

The story takes place _____

_____

_____

The main characters in the story are _____

_____

_____

A problem occurs when _____

_____

_____

After that, _____

_____

_____

_____

_____

The problem is solved when _____

_____

_____

▶ PCM 3

Problem/Solution Work Sheet

1. What is the problem? _____

_____

_____

2. What causes the problem? _____

_____

_____

_____

3. What are some possible solutions? _____

_____

_____

_____

_____

_____

4. What is the best solution? Why is it the best? _____

_____

_____

_____

_____

Cause-and-Effect Chart

List causes and effects in the appropriate boxes. For a cause-and-effect chain, draw an arrow from the effect box down to the next cause box.

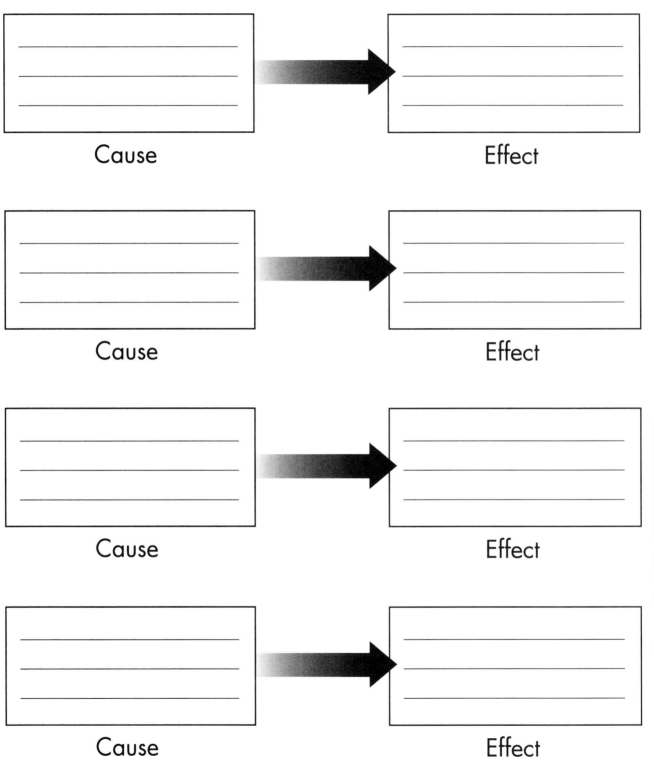

Comparison/Contrast Grid

Use this grid to compare and contrast two people or things. Write the names of the two subjects in the title and as the headings of the two middle columns. List the topics, or issues, you are going to compare and contrast in the first column. Write the contrasts, or differences, in the middle columns. Write the comparisons, or similarities, in the column labeled *Both*.

Comparison and Contrast of _____

Topic or Issue	Subject 1 _____	Subject 2 _____	Both

Idea Map

Write your topic on the line below. In the center circle, write a topic sentence summarizing your opinion about the topic. In the surrounding circles, list examples or reasons that support your topic sentence. You can add more circles if you'd like.

My Topic _____

Example or reason
that supports my opinion

_____

_____

_____

_____

Example or reason
that supports my opinion

_____

_____

_____

_____

My opinion
(topic sentence)

_____

_____

_____

_____

Example or reason
that supports my opinion

_____

_____

_____

_____

Example or reason
that supports my opinion

_____

_____

_____

_____

Strategies for Recognizing Words

Here are some tips for recognizing unfamiliar words when you read.

Tip 1: Try another pronunciation.
If your first pronunciation didn't make sense, try another one. You will probably recognize the word when you get it right. Check whether your guess makes sense in the sentence or the paragraph. Then check your guess in a dictionary.

Tip 2: Use context clues.
Look for clues to the word in the context—the surrounding sentences and paragraph. Ask, "What word starts with these letters and would make sense in this context?" Make a guess. Check whether your guess makes sense. Then check your guess in the dictionary.

Tip 3: Divide compound words into their smaller whole words.
If the unknown word has smaller words that you recognize, divide it into the smaller words. Read the smaller words. Then read them together. Check that the compound word makes sense in the context.

Examples: when/ever   over/heard   waste/basket   summer/time

Tip 4: Divide words with roots, prefixes, and suffixes into those parts.
If the unknown word has a root and prefixes or suffixes, divide the word into those parts. Read the root first. Then add the prefixes and/or suffixes to read the whole word. Check that the word makes sense in the context.

Some common prefixes and suffixes	Examples in words
prefixes: de-, in-, ex-, re-, per-, sub-, trans-	de/pend, re/flect, sub/tract
suffixes: -able, -ful, -ion, -or, -ous	nerv/ous, pollut/ion, in/ex/cus/able

Tip 5: Divide long words into syllables.

	Examples
• A syllable must have one vowel sound.	trou/ble, straight/en
• Divide between vowels that have separate sounds.	di/et, so/ci/e/ty

• Do not divide vowel pairs that make one sound.
    a. Long vowel pairs: *ai, ee, ea, oa, oo*
    b. Other vowel pairs: *au, oi, oy, ou*
	in/crease, con/tain/er
	daugh/ter, poi/son

• Divide between double consonants.	in/ter/rupt, pos/si/ble
• Divide before a consonant plus *le* at the end of a word.	am/ple, re/spon/si/ble

Student Progress Tracking Sheet

Name: _____

Lesson: _____

Date started: _____ Date ended: _____

What I learned from the reading: _____

_____

_____

What I learned from **Think About It:** _____

_____

What I learned from **Write About It:** _____

_____

What I learned from the **Life Skill:** _____

_____

_____

What I liked best about the lesson: _____

_____

_____

What I need more practice with: _____

_____

_____

Tips for Preparing a Progress Portfolio

Your Progress Portfolio will show what you have learned in the period covered by this portfolio. Follow these tips as you prepare your portfolio.

1. Photocopy your completed Student Self-Assessment. Put it in your Progress Portfolio folder.

2. Gather all of the Student Progress Tracking Sheets that you have completed for the period. Put them in your portfolio folder.

3. Choose the samples of your writing that you would like to put in your portfolio. Make sure your name, a title, and the date it was written are on each writing sample.

4. List the writing samples you chose for your portfolio. Tell why you chose each one. Put the list and the samples in your portfolio.

5. Look at all the other material in your working folder. Pick out the items you would like to include in your Progress Portfolio. List these items and tell why you chose each one. Put the list and the items in your portfolio.

6. Think about the skills you have learned. List the skills pages you would like to include in your portfolio:

Think About It pages: _____

_____

Life Skill pages: _____

_____

Writing Skills Mini-Lesson pages: _____

_____

Photocopy these pages. Make sure your name and a date are on each page. Make a separate list of the pages you are putting in your portfolio. Put the list and the photocopies in your folder.

7. Look through the materials in your portfolio folder. Read the questions on PCM 11. Think about answers to these questions as you prepare for your portfolio conference.

Portfolio Conference Questionnaire

To the Instructor: Use this questionnaire as you conduct portfolio conferences with students.

Student: _____ Date: _____

Instructor: _____ Course: _____

1. Which writing samples and skills pages have you chosen for your portfolio?

2. Why did you choose these items?

3. What do these items show you that you have learned?

4. What selections are you most proud of? Why?

5. What would you like to do better?

6. What would you like to do more of?

7. What do you still need to do to reach your educational goals?

▶ PCM 11